GET YOUR KIDS TO EAT ANYTHING

An Hachette UK Company
www.hachette.co.uk

First published in Great Britain in 2019 by
Mitchell Beazley,
an imprint of Octopus Publishing Group Ltd
Carmelite House, 50 Victoria Embankment
London EC4Y 0DZ
www.octopusbooks.co.uk

Distributed in the US by Hachette Book Group
1290 Avenue of the Americas
4th and 5th Floors
New York, NY 10104

Distributed in Canada by Canadian Manda Group
664 Annette St.
Toronto, Ontario, Canada M6S 2C8

ISBN 978-1-78472-558-7

A CIP catalogue record for this book is available from
the British Library.

Printed and bound in China

10 9 8 7 6 5 4 3 2 1

Editorial Director Eleanor Maxfield
Junior Editor Ella Parsons
Copy Editor Lucy Bannell
Senior Designer Jaz Bahra
Photographer Tom Regester
Illustrator Ella Mclean
Food Stylist Becks Wilkinson
Prop Stylist Agathe Gits
Make-up Artist Dominika Kasperowicz
Production Manager Lisa Pinnell

Both imperial and metric measurements have been
given in all recipes. Use one set of measurements
only and not a mixture of both.

Standard level spoon measurements are used in
all recipes.
1 tablespoon = one 15 ml spoon
1 teaspoon = one 5 ml spoon

Fresh herbs should be used unless otherwise stated.

For US egg sizes, choose a size larger than given in
a recipe: a UK medium egg is a US large egg; a UK
large egg is a US extra-large egg.

GET YOUR KIDS TO EAT ANYTHING

THE 5-PHASE PROGRAMME TO CHANGE
THE WAY YOUR FAMILY THINKS ABOUT FOOD

EMILY LEARY

MITCHELL BEAZLEY

For Mark, JD and Jay.

And for my mum, who taught me everything I know and without whose encouragement this book would not exist.

CONTENTS

Introduction

THE PHILOSOPHY

"He used to love broccoli, now he won't touch it. We're down to the last couple of veg he will eat."

"If it's not beige, she won't even allow it on the plate."

"Beans were her favourite last week but now she's beside herself because there's one bean in her spaghetti hoops."

"They love vegetables at nursery, but at home they will only eat fish fingers."

Familiar? How about these:

"We're so busy, we just tend to eat the same meals most weeks."

"I don't want mealtimes to be a battle, so we stick to the dishes we know we all like."

"I sometimes end up making a different dinner for every member of the family."

These are extremely common comments I hear time and time again, both as a parent and in my years working in family food. I've made more than a few of them myself.

Fussy and picky eating in children is completely normal and can happen for all sorts of reasons. They might be feeling under the weather, they might just be at the "no" stage, they might have got comfortable with a diet of treat food during a family holiday. They might have reasons that, in their minds, seem totally rational – to them, not wanting to eat their soup because it has "green dots" (herbs) in it might seem totally sensible.

Whatever the reasons, in the vast majority of cases it's completely possible to bring children to (or back to) a healthy, adventurous attitude to food.

In my experience of feeding children (a seven-year-old daughter with a long history of chronic throat infections and an 11-year-old son on the autistic spectrum), I've learned that unfamiliar colours, aromas, textures or flavours present the most regular mealtime challenges. If it doesn't look, smell, feel or taste the way they're used to, it can be quickly rejected. We've all cried, more than once, "How do you know if you haven't even tried it?" – right?

Even a familiar food presented in an unfamiliar way can cause issues, such as if your family are used to breaded fish, but you serve it "naked". Or you bake pink salmon when they're used to white cod. Neophobia, or fear of the new, is a very natural stage most children go through, but if it becomes a long-term habit, their diets can become extremely limited.

A few years ago, I was facing my own challenges with our family's food. I've always enjoyed cooking, but before I had children I had my five favourite meals and we ate them again and again. We were stuck in a rut, but we didn't really care.

Then our son was born and there were feeding challenges: he was badly jaundiced, my milk didn't come in well, then he was diagnosed with a dairy allergy (which, thankfully, he has grown out of). Challenge after challenge meant it was such a delight when, at six months, we could finally introduce him to solids. And he loved puréed veg – it was all going to be easy from here on...

And it was for a while – feeding a baby isn't so challenging because no one really expects them to eat a huge variety of meals. As he grew into an active toddler, JD settled on certain foods he liked and I was happy to make them for him. But then came a point where it was near-impossible to introduce him to anything new at all.

One day, my mum was visiting while JD was eating dinner. Quite off the cuff, she observed that everything he loved to eat the most was orange. And she was right!

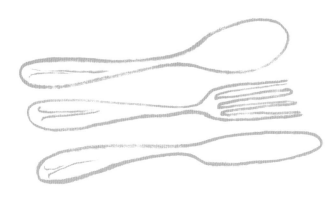

His favourite meals were sure to feature butternut squash, sweet potato, carrots or swede. These are all healthy vegetables, of course, but it was a flag that made me realize his concept of what made a food palatable was narrowing.

After that, the evidence stacked up that he was becoming reliant on food being predictable, the same, normal. Grocery orders looked the same week after week. I could practically make his favourite meals with my eyes closed.

But who can blame any child for being suspicious of new foods? Imagine walking up to someone who has lived their whole life seeing only red, round apples and offering them a blue, triangular one. You could tell them all you like that it tastes just as good as a regular apple... but would they believe you? Perhaps not.

When we serve the same ingredients cooked in the same way in the same combination time and time again, we set very narrow "rules" in our subconscious – and in that of our children – about what "normal" looks like, and it becomes natural to reject what's new or different.

My son would eye new foods with suspicion and, although I would try to introduce dishes to him, after minimal success – and through fear of him not getting enough nutrition – I would go back to a few days of reliable meals before trying something else. No luck. There were times I felt that he was holding out and waiting for me to give in. If you've ever had a child reject their favourite meal purely because you cooked it slightly differently, you're probably nodding along.

I realized that if we really wanted to make this work, we needed to stick with it. Almost like taking up a new form of exercise, the hard part isn't the exercise itself, it's sticking with it long enough so that it becomes a

habit. And a healthy approach to meals certainly wasn't going to become a habit for our son if we didn't do it consistently.

And that's when I hit upon the approach that is at the core of this book. If "new" was at the root of my son's fear of variety, then it was the routine that must change to **make new the norm**. If, from day to day, his food varied so much that he never had the chance to get set in his ways, then trying something unfamiliar would become expected and therefore comfortable.

Tentatively, I began to serve different ingredients cooked in different ways in different combinations. I set myself a challenge that for an indeterminate

period – maybe a week, maybe a month, maybe a year – I would never serve quite the same meal cooked in exactly the same way twice in a row. Metaphorically, if my family had eaten green apples and buttered pink toast for breakfast on Monday, then I was going to grate triangular blue apples into our green porridge on Tuesday.

Conscious that I wanted to foster a love of food, not put JD off entirely, I started with small changes – a pinch of curry spice added to otherwise familiar mashed potato, a few lentils in our favourite spaghetti bolognese – and worked up to new ingredients and dishes gently over time.

Within the limits of real life and all its challenges, I continued to change things up often, never serving the same meal in quite the same way twice, and – gradually – the resistance fell away and things changed dramatically for the better.

By the time JD turned three, I was pregnant with our daughter, Jay, and on maternity leave. With more time to enjoy at home, I decided to set up a blog, A Mummy Too, to record our mother-son adventures and our shared love of food.

What started out as a sort of online diary quickly became a place for our recipes, activities and tips. JD's appetite for new flavours and textures was expanding, while Jay was embarking on the same journey, so I was able to share new dishes as we discovered and cooked them. And readers started to find my blog and cook the same recipes, too.

I continued to blog after going back to work full time and carried on receiving messages from other parents who were balancing work and parenting while doing their best to feed their families interesting, healthy, varied meals.

By now, the blog was receiving thousands of visits a day and I was becoming increasingly passionate about documenting our foodie adventures. In 2014, three years after I began blogging, I quit my day job and in the months that followed, A Mummy Too became a multi-award-winning online reference for busy parents. I had found my true passion.

Going full time with the blog allowed me to give more attention to developing new meals, testing new ideas and keeping an eye on how our family ate. When our busy lives, unwell kids or all manner of other life challenges knocked our food habits off course, the process of getting them back on track meant I was able to hone my understanding of what makes a family resistant or receptive to new foods.

And after years of trialling and refining the process, falling back into old habits and overcoming setbacks, I know what works for us, and that is what I'm sharing with you now.

Through five key phases, you are going to gradually change how your family thinks about food. You are going to **make new the norm** and enjoy healthy, varied meals that the whole family will enjoy.

MORE THAN A RECIPE BOOK

In this book, you'll find 70 family-friendly, unusual, sometimes challenging and always delicious recipes, but this is *not* a recipe book.

You're about to be introduced to a whole new approach to family meals, a "how to" guide for parents in the ongoing struggle to overcome picky eating and **make new the norm**.

Over the next 200 pages, we'll be embarking on an adventure to change the way you and your family look at food and to bring healthy variety into every meal for years to come, far beyond the recipes you discover within this book.

You will ease away from the same four to six staple meals most families fall back on, toward truly varied recipes and meal plans from day to day, week to week, to the point where introducing your whole family to new flavours, colours and textures is a breeze because **new is the norm**.

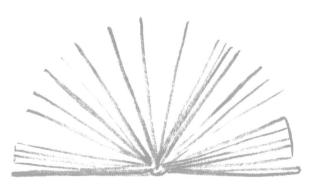

THE 5-PHASE APPROACH

Of course, changing a lifetime of food habits isn't as simple as just varying what you put on the table, so your journey is divided into key phases:

Phase 1: Put the unfamiliar into the familiar

Start gently with variety at mealtimes. Begin to introduce small elements of unfamiliar colour, flavour or texture into family favourites. Think lentil bolognese, or curried fish and chips.

Phase 2: Educate

Experiment with texture, taste and smell, and look into the science of taste. Understand where your food comes from and why that's important. And build a relationship with food through growing your own.

3

Phase 3: Discover the fun in food

Put the enjoyment back into food by making each meal an occasion. Overcome visual resistance to certain foods and build a new level of enthusiasm for variety with arty plates and creative, exciting dishes, such as bright red risotto.

4

Phase 4: Step into the unknown

Discover ingredients and flavour combinations that will be surprising even to grown-up palates. Push food boundaries in delicious ways, such as with strawberries and cream pasta!

5

Phase 5: Cement variety

You've come so far and experimented with a wide range of new flavours. Now it's time to make sure the habit sticks. Learn techniques to keep your family mealtimes varied long term.

Each phase includes an explanation of what you're going to learn and achieve, clear advice and two weeks of delicious tried-and-tested recipes. Scattered throughout the book are hands-on food activities to try out with your children, all of which will help you and your family to progress.

The phases are designed to be worked through chronologically, but there's no set time over which you should tackle each one. You could whizz through the whole book in ten weeks or tackle it more gently over a few months.

If you feel ready to jump ahead to a particular recipe, or if an activity from another phase catches your eye, that's fine. And if you decide to move backward to work some more on a past phase, that's fine too.

Every family is different and it's important that the process is always enjoyable and never a chore.

PREPARING TO BEGIN

In each phase, you'll be given a two-week meal plan. During that two weeks, 14 meals will be planned for you, with blank slots left for you to fill in the remaining meals. You'll probably find it works best to plan and shop at the start of each week – refer to pages 215–19 for bespoke shopping lists to support each phase.

INGREDIENTS TO STOCK UP ON

To get you stocked up for the weeks ahead, and to help you get into the habit of making healthy choices when preparing meals to fill those free option slots in your meal plans, I've compiled a list of delicious and healthy core ingredients to use as the basis for some great, varied meals.

I've left out the obvious essentials, such as bread, milk and pasta.

CUPBOARD ESSENTIALS

These are the items you'll reach for time and time again. With long shelf lives, they'll sit ready and waiting for the right meal to come along.

- **Oil** – A cooking essential. Grab a bottle of flavourless oil (such as sunflower oil), a bottle of olive oil and an oil spray so you're all set for hot and cold food prep.

- **Butter** – Invaluable for adding a rich, creamy taste to almost everything, as well as structure to baked goods, butter also has a low smoking point that makes browning foods in a pan super easy.

- **Flour** – With a bag each of plain flour, wholewheat flour, self-raising flour and strong bread flour, you'll be set for most baking challenges, from breakfast to dinner, starters to desserts.

- **Baking bits** – Pick up some tubs of bicarbonate of soda, baking powder and fast-action dried yeast and you'll find that you rarely need to go shopping when you want to try out a new baking recipe.

- **Canned tomatoes** – Tomatoes will open up hundreds of options for you, acting as the key that transforms a random collection of meat and veg into a stew, bolognese, chilli or curry. Grab a can or tube of tomato purée too, for when you want concentrated flavour.

- **Honey** – A fantastic ingredient that adds a wonderful depth of flavour to both savoury and sweet dishes. Sweeter than sugar but twice as tasty, honey should always be in your cupboard.

- **Rice** – A bag of brown rice, a bag of white rice and you're ready to bulk out delicious recipes with an ingredient enjoyed by millions (if not billions) of people every day.

- **Canned beans** – Grab a can each of the following: haricot, kidney, butter, black and cannellini beans. Try swapping out other proteins in your meal for beans instead – you'll be amazed at what you can do with a humble can.

- **Alternative grains** – You've probably already got pasta in store, which is great! Now stock your cupboards with quinoa, rye, barley and freekeh, and try using them in dishes you would normally make with couscous, pasta or rice.

- **Dried beans, peas and lentils** – These can bulk out all sorts of meals with healthy proteins. Grab a selection.

- **Chickpeas** – A bag of dried chickpeas and a few cans of chickpeas in water will last for months and are great for whizzing up a quick hummus, adding substance to a curry, or tossing over a salad.

- **Stock** – Homemade or from a cube, a good stock can enliven any dish. Aim to pick up the low-salt versions, if you can.

- **Dried breadcrumbs** – For coating and frying, breadcrumbs are a great way of getting a crunch on items such as breaded fish or Scotch eggs. To make breadcrumbs, simply put some lightly toasted bread into a food processor and blitz until fine.

- **Condiments** – An easy way of adding a quick hit of flavour. You no doubt already have mayonnaise and ketchup in stock, but grab some Worcestershire sauce, sriracha, sweet chilli and Tabasco too, so that you're ready to introduce lots of variation to your cooking.

- **Garlic** – Adds its pungent, unmistakable flavour to dishes throughout the world. If a savoury dish is missing something you can't quite put your finger on, it may well be garlic.

REFRIGERATOR

- **Cheese** – You don't have to ditch the Cheddar, but having a few varieties of cheese will open up loads of new cooking options. A hard cheese such as Parmesan can lend a lovely warm depth of flavour to sauces, while packaged mozzarella and goats' cheese can liven up everything from salad to savoury bakes.

- **Chillies** – These can do everything, from acting as the star of the show, to adding a subtle hint of warmth. They're a fantastic way of mixing up a dish and challenging young taste buds.

- **Eggs** – Humble, but delicious in their own right, whether poached, scrambled or fried, and easy to build a host of fantastic dishes around. What's more, the unique binding quality of eggs makes them invaluable in baking.

- **Fruit** – Have a good selection of fruit to hand, including at least one or two items you wouldn't normally buy.

- **Vegetables** – Always have a variety of vegetables in the refrigerator. However, if you have more than three different types in stock that you haven't got a plan for, don't buy any more until you've used up what you have.

- **Yogurt** – From Greek- and Indian-spiced dishes, to sweet desserts and breakfasts, yogurt is an essential part of many recipes and great on its own, too.

SPICES

There are probably a few spices you use regularly, but you will be introduced to some key ones in this book and discover new ways of using them. The spices below will all be used at least once during the coming weeks. Go out and grab them all.

- **Cayenne** – With its mellow, chilli-like aroma and powerful punch, cayenne can make a good chilli great.

- **Cinnamon** – Fruity, sweet and warm, cinnamon is great in porridge, delightful with apples and incredible in spicy Mexican dishes.

- **Cumin** – Light, almost floral, with a hint of grass, cumin will add a distinctive flavour.

- **Mustard** – Rich and earthy tones combined with a slight sweetness and a kick on the tongue, mustard adds piquancy to creamy sauces, salad dressings and more.

- **Paprika** – Earthy and rich with a slightly aged taste, paprika can add warmth without heat.

- **Turmeric** – Floral and sometimes slightly bitter, turmeric is essential to a good curry and adds a fantastic golden hue.

- **Vanilla** – Be it from a pod or a bottle of extract, a little vanilla adds a distinctive rounded aroma and taste that enhances sweet dishes.

HERBS

An easy addition to your cooking, dried herbs add aromatic variation without being overpowering. (In Phase 2, you'll learn how to turn some cheap plants from the supermarket into your very own herb garden.)

- **Basil** – Lively, aromatic and peppery, basil is the perfect partner to tomatoes.

- **Chives** – Tangy and fresh with a mellow, onion-like flavour, chives can lift potatoes, salads and more to a whole new level.

- **Mint** – Light, leafy and refreshing, mint beautifully complements fruit, chocolate and lamb.

- **Oregano** – With a warm, dense taste, oregano is a dream addition to Mediterranean dishes.

- **Parsley** – Mildly bitter with a grassy flavour, parsley will add a freshness to your dish.

- **Sage** – Floral and woody with a slightly bitter taste, sage can add a meaty element to vegetable dishes.

- **Thyme** – With its light earthiness and floral aroma, thyme makes roast potatoes taste incredible and can be pretty special in some fruit dishes, too.

NUTS AND SEEDS

These offer a wonderful opportunity to lift the texture and flavour of a dish. They're also great for snacking, and nutritionally rich, offering a host of omega oils and vitamins. Here are some of my favourites.

- **Almonds** – These offer a distinctive flavour and crunchy texture that's perfect for snacking.

- **Cashews** – With a creamy texture and mild flavour, cashews are great in stir-fries.

- **Pine nuts** – Raw or toasted, pine nuts add a gorgeous, warm taste to pizza, pasta and more. I love them sprinkled on a cake before baking to create an incredible crust.

- **Pumpkin seeds** – Mild, soft and nutty, I toss pumpkin seeds into salads and stir-fries, or sprinkle them over stews and pasta dishes.

- **Sunflower seeds** – With a crisp shell and the flavour of a mild nut, sunflower seeds are wonderful sprinkled on salads, kneaded into dough or stirred into cereal.

- **Walnuts** – These complement fruit and cheese beautifully. Once you start adding them to dishes, you won't want to stop.

FREEZER STAPLES

- **Frozen fruit and veg** – I always have a whole freezer drawer full of frozen fruit and veg. Sure, fresh produce is great, but when time simply won't allow, frozen does the job and is still nutritionally beneficial. And it also means you can enjoy seasonal produce, such as summer berries, all year round.

- **Frozen ready-rolled pastry** – Pastry can form the basis for a wide range of interesting meals, but it's not always something we have time to make from scratch. Having pastry in the freezer means a lack of time won't present a barrier to a great meal.

ADJUSTING YOUR MINDSET, PREPARING YOUR FAMILY

I hope you are excited to begin, but a little trepidation is quite normal. Before we dive in, here are some tips to help get you started on the right foot. These are ideas you can start to introduce into meals today to begin to lay the foundations for the journey ahead.

Fear not, we'll tackle many of these concepts and more in far greater depth as we progress through the five different phases, but this will give you a taste of what's to come.

IF YOU'RE INVESTED, YOUR CHILDREN WILL BE TOO

Leading by example is hugely important, since children acquire behaviours from the significant role models around them.

I'm a big vegetable fan, so my plate is always piled high with greens, but my husband will be the first to admit that he was not really keen on salad or veg before we met. He wasn't veg-phobic, but if he was making a meal for himself, the chances of anything green appearing on the plate were pretty slim. And then he became a dad and we realized that, if we expected the kids to eat a healthy, balanced diet, everyone else at the table needed to do the same.

During this journey (and hopefully beyond), take care to express positive emotions, verbally and non-verbally, around the food you are enjoying together. It will go a long way.

TOO MUCH CHOICE CAN BE COUNTERPRODUCTIVE

I'm really not a believer in telling a child to eat what they are given or starve, but I do think that too much choice can leave them in a spin. This is especially true if they're the type of child who, like my son, often thinks there's a right answer that you're expecting them to give. Avoid open questions such as, "What do you want to eat?" and instead aim for just a couple of choices, both of which add up to a balanced plate.

INTRODUCE THE "NO PLATE WITHOUT VEG" RULE

When my husband and I both found ourselves particularly busy with work, we realized we were often grabbing a bowl of canned soup or a quick sandwich. Our five a day was looking more like 0.5 a day.

We realized it was also impacting on how we were feeding the kids. "Spaghetti on toast, you say, kids? Awesome! That only takes five minutes!" So we made a quick family rule that you can't have a plate without salad or veg on it. You can have a sandwich, canned soup or something else quick now and then, but there always has to be some veg on the plate.

More often than not, I realized that if I was getting out the veg for the side of the plate, I might as well put a quick casserole or veg-packed pasta together, so this rule generally keeps us on the right track.

TRY NOT TO SHOW YOUR STRESS

There was a period a couple of years ago when our daughter's throat was really sore every other week and, probably as a consequence, she didn't want anything other than pasta in a creamy sauce. No veg, no variety and just one colour: beige.

After a few weeks, we really started to worry about malnutrition and how it would affect her long term. Then one day, I heard myself trying to talk her round to a different meal and my voice was strained, maybe even a little shrill. I was ignoring all my best advice and letting my worries pass on to her. That day, we paused, took a breath and went back to square one. We slowly introduced more challenging colours and textures until she was more comfortable again.

The lesson we learned was that a lot of fussy eating can be down to underlying worries or fears. It's vital that you work to support and dispel those, rather than contribute to them. No two children are alike, but with a relaxed, positive attitude, working through the five phases should be pleasurable and rewarding for all.

INVOLVE THE KIDS IN THE COOKING PROCESS

Have you ever put plates of lovingly prepared, healthy food in front of the kids only for their eyes to widen in horror as they ask, "What *is* it?" Yes, me too. And it stings!

I've figured out over the years that it really helps to have the kids involved in making their own meals. Whether it's grating cheese, stirring ingredients, kneading bread or pouring pie fillings into their cases, they're much more likely to be comfortable with the finished result if they've seen what goes into it. Plus, of course, if they've helped along the way, they'll hopefully feel proud enough of their efforts to want to enjoy their food.

You'll notice that I've included plenty of child-friendly elements in the preparation of the recipes throughout this book, so they should have plenty to do. Be sure to keep that whole-family involvement going. And, most importantly, enjoy the process!

WHY IT PAYS TO MEAL PLAN

Imagine standing, ravenous and exhausted, in a supermarket at 6pm. What would you pick up for dinner? Easy, quick, filling options, no doubt. Now imagine shopping calmly, quietly, stomach full, head clear. What might you buy then? Healthier options, I'm guessing, and perhaps ingredients for slightly more ambitious dishes too.

The fact is, it's typically easier for us to make healthier, more balanced choices when we are given the time and space to do so. Meal planning can even save you money, since you buy only what you need and can shop strategically. I save a small fortune by buying reduced-price items from the supermarket – there's no danger in buying food that is almost past its use-by date if your meal plan tells you it will all be cooked within a safe time. And I save hours too, since I no longer have to make daily dashes to the supermarket for last-minute ingredients.

I like to meal plan on a Saturday or Sunday. I sit down, usually in the evening after the kids are in bed, and set out roughly what we're likely to eat in the week ahead. When I started out, I focused mainly on evening meals, but as time passed, I realized it was easy to build in breakfasts and lunches too. So think about what you've eaten as a family this week. Take a look in the refrigerator, in the cupboard. How much needs chucking out because you bought it on a whim and never got around to cooking it? With meal planning, you're going to get a better handle on your family's eating habits than ever before.

In developing the meal plans for this book, I put a lot of thought into how much cooking and planning busy parents like me can realistically fit into their day, and how that can translate into meaningfully healthy eating patterns for the long term.

Having spoken to lots of fellow parents, there's general agreement that evening meals are the biggest challenge, particularly as many children are at school or nursery during the day, while time is limited in the evenings.

But parents also acknowledge that breakfasts can easily become repetitive and weekends are when they're most likely to have a little more time to cook.

For this reason, the weekly meal plans in each phase of this book are each made up of one or two breakfasts, three or four evening meals and two weekend lunches. The rest is up to you. These plans and the recipes within them are flexible because only you know the unique challenges placed upon your family's availability. Move things around, add or swap portions of veg or meat as you see fit, make the most of leftovers and add ideas to keep your family engaged, while making the best use of your time.

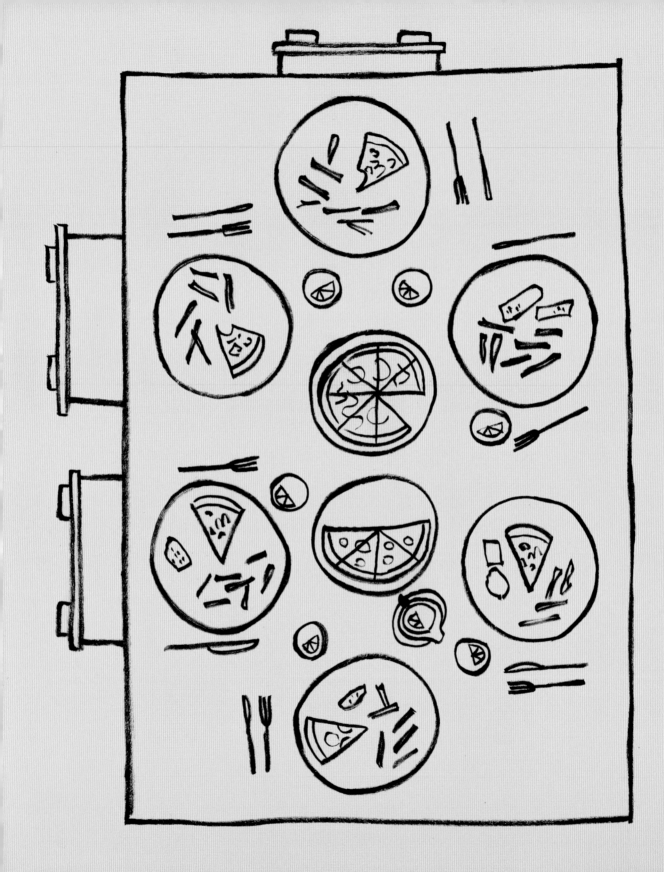

PHASE 1

Put the unfamiliar into the familiar

During this first phase, we're going to take some trusted family favourites and change them just enough so that we start experimenting with variety. We're going to add spice to some classically bland dishes. We're going to add crunch and colour to dishes that are typically beige and smooth. We are going to start to break some early assumptions about what food "should" be like *just* enough to get all of you excited about the journey ahead.

Remember, as you begin Phase 1, that we're not embarking on a battle with our families. This is not about forcing unpleasant food upon them in the name of variety. These are delicious, wholesome, enjoyable meals.

Sometimes reactions may be mixed, sometimes your cooking will go down a storm. Sometimes you'll want to revisit recipes that were rejected first time round, sometimes the kids will ask for the same things over and over again, but with a little persistence and patience, you'll all have fun.

DECONSTRUCTING MEALTIMES

TASK 1: HOW TO MAKE NEW THE NORM

Grab pencil and paper and jot down what you usually eat for breakfast. Now write down your family's typical lunches. And finally, make a note of the top three evening meals you tend to have most weeks.

My guess is that this wasn't a particularly challenging task. Most parents could reel off the answers without skipping a beat. Everyone has favourite meals, and enjoying them is one of life's greatest pleasures, one that shouldn't be underestimated. On this journey, we're not trying to eliminate favourites. Instead, we're aiming to tackle the degree of repetition that can overwhelm your family mealtimes and threaten to make introducing new flavours, textures and ingredients almost impossible.

So how do we start to introduce variety gently? For me, it starts with picturing a tried-and-tested dish and then changing something about it. For example, if you're a family of porridge fans, how about grating an apple on top, or adding berries to the oats as they cook? If you're set on sandwiches as your family lunch of choice, how about making the swap from sliced bread to tortillas?

If you find that you're hitting a dead end with new ideas, stick with me. I'm going to show you how I like to break down a meal into its component food groups so it's easy to see what could be swapped, tweaked, taken out, added in or made healthier...or even flipped completely on its head.

Let's use classic fish fingers with chips and peas as an example.

DESCRIBE THE MEAL AS IF TO SOMEONE WHO HAS NEVER HEARD OF IT

Fish fingers are usually made from a white, non-oily fish.

Could we use a different type of fish?

They are cut into strips about the length of a finger.

Could we cut the shapes differently?

They are coated in breadcrumbs.

Could we flavour the breadcrumbs?
Could we marinate the fish?
Might we add spice?

And then they are baked, grilled or fried.

Could we cook them differently?

The chips are made from white potato.

Could we use a different potato?
Could we use another vegetable completely?
How could we add flavour?

The potato is usually cut into thin strips.

Could we cut the potato differently?

The strips are then either baked or fried with oil.

Could we cook them differently?

DESCRIBE THE MEAL IN TERMS OF ITS MAIN NUTRITIONAL GROUPS

CARBOHYDRATE:
THE POTATO CHIPS, THE BREADCRUMBS

Carbs make up a large part of the meal. Could I reduce the number of chips? What other carbs could replace the potato?

PROTEIN:
WHITE FISH

Could meat also be cut into fingers? What about vegetable proteins? Could I use oily fish, such as salmon?

FRUIT AND VEGETABLES:
USUALLY SERVED WITH PEAS

How could we add flavour to the peas? What other vegetable could we add to the plate?

FATTY AND SUGARY FOODS:
OIL IF THE CHIPS ARE FRIED

How can we avoid frying in oil, but still have flavour?

DAIRY:
NONE

What kinds of dairy might complement the fish and chips? As there's no dairy on the plate, could I factor it into dessert?

DESCRIBE THE MEAL IN TERMS OF ITS COLOURS

BEIGE:
CHIPS

Could I change the colour with spices? What if I tried a different type of potato?

ORANGE-BEIGE:
FISH FINGERS

How could I achieve an orange colour in a way that tastes good? Shall I aim for a totally different colour?

GREEN:
PEAS

How can I add more colour? Shall I include more vegetables?

DESCRIBE THE MEAL IN TERMS OF ITS FLAVOURS

SWEET? *A little sweetness from the peas.*
SALTY? *Perhaps, if the chips are salted.*
BITTER? *No.*
SOUR? *No.*
SAVOURY? *Yes.*
SPICY? *No.*

I can see that the flavour profile of the meal is very simple. Could I add more sweetness, spice or other flavours?

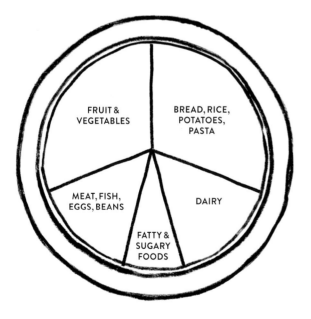

TASK 2: RETHINK FISH FINGERS AND CHIPS

Try to come up with your own tweaked version of fish
fingers and chips. Here's a table for you to use when
considering how to vary your meals. When you're done,
see page 33 to see how closely your ideas match my own.

	MY ANSWERS	MY IDEAS
DESCRIBE THE MEAL AS IF TO SOMEONE WHO HAS NEVER HEARD OF IT		
DESCRIBE THE MEAL IN TERMS OF ITS MAIN NUTRITIONAL GROUPS Carbs (bread, rice, potatoes, pasta)? Protein (meat, fish, eggs, beans)? Fruit and vegetables? Fatty and sugary foods? Dairy?		
DESCRIBE THE MEAL IN TERMS OF ITS COLOURS		
DESCRIBE THE MEAL IN TERMS OF ITS FLAVOURS Sweet? Salty? Bitter? Sour? Savoury? Spicy?		

TASK 3: GET CHILDREN INTERESTED IN NUTRITION

When our eldest son was about two years old, he came home from nursery one day having learned about healthy balanced diets. The impact the session had on him was unmistakable. He was full of new-found enthusiasm for what was on his plate. He wanted to know what nutritional group each element of his dinner fell into and how it contributed to the healthy functioning of his body.

"Is this protein? Which vitamins are in carrots?
Did you know too much fat is bad?
Do we eat our five a day?"

This was an exciting moment for me. His nursery key worker had started a fire in him and his passion for healthy food was burning bright. Now the challenge was to keep that fire alight. And it was hit-and-miss, I have to confess, but we learned a lot along the way.

So that's the challenge I want to begin with you. Let's learn some facts and come away with a long-lasting passion for healthy, varied, exciting meals.

First, take a look at the balanced plate on page 25. If you haven't already, now is a great time to look at it together with your kids, study it, encourage them to ask questions.

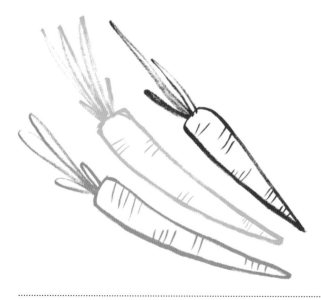

TASK 4: KITCHEN HUNT

Raid the kitchen cupboards and the refrigerator with the kids, make a list of all the items you can find and note which category they belong to.

GROUP	WHAT WE FOUND
CARBOHYDRATE	
PROTEIN	
DAIRY	
FRUIT AND VEG	
FATTY / SUGARY	

Were there any items that seemed to belong to more than one category? Did the labels give you any clues?

Next, sit down and try to form a real-life healthy plate diagram together. You might create a wedge out of pasta, one from a chunk of cheese, some carrots for the vegetables and so on. Now, with your children's interest in varied food piqued, it's time to start cooking!

PHASE 1 RECIPES

I hope you're excited to get started with the first 14 recipes on your journey to bringing habitual variety to your family mealtimes. You're going to start by shaking up breakfast with a delicious smoothie that tastes like apple pie, before moving through a host of familiar meals, such as pizza, burger, fish and chips, shepherd's pie and pasta bake, but all with an exciting twist.

Once you've tried each recipe, fill in the reflection journal on pages 58–59 to record your family's thoughts about each meal. What was their initial reaction? What did they like? What would you like to change next time?

These recipes are not just designed to be different, they've also been tested and retested to ensure they're tasty! Some children and adults will take to this new-found variety quickly and enthusiastically, but, for the more reluctant eaters, remember that adapting to new flavours and textures can take time, so you might want to revisit some of these recipes again in the future.

Good luck and let's get cooking!

Phase 1 meal plans

Here are your first two weekly meal plans, pre-filled with every recipe you'll be making during Phase 1, organized so that you can see at a glance what you'll be cooking and when.

Fill in the blanks yourself. Challenge yourself to add at least one new idea per day, in addition to the supplied recipes. If you're popping in old favourites, remember to think about how you could add or change one element of each meal to make a familiar dish into something new.

And remember to look across the days as a whole to see how balanced your daily intake looks: does protein feature? Is there room to add another portion of fruit or veg?

WEEK 1

	BREAKFAST	LUNCH	DINNER
MONDAY	APPLE PIE SMOOTHIE		
TUESDAY			CURRIED FISH FINGERS WITH SWEET POTATO CHIPS
WEDNESDAY			CHILLI BEAN BURGERS
THURSDAY			RAINBOW PIZZA
FRIDAY			CHICKEN AND VEGETABLE BLACK NOODLE STIR-FRY
SATURDAY		SPINACH "MEATBALL" PASTA BAKE	
SUNDAY		PUY LENTIL SHEPHERD'S PIE	

WEEK 2

	BREAKFAST	LUNCH	DINNER
MONDAY	BREAKFAST FRITTATA		
TUESDAY			BAKED POTATO WITH CHUNKY HOMEMADE BAKED BEANS
WEDNESDAY			CHILLI CON CARNE-STUFFED PEPPERS
THURSDAY			LENTIL SPAGHETTI BOLOGNESE
FRIDAY			MINTY-CITRUS PESTO PASTA WITH EDAMAME
SATURDAY		VEG-PACKED BEEF BURGERS	
SUNDAY		VEGGIE TOAD-IN-THE-HOLE	

PREP TIME: 10 MINS

Apple pie smoothie

This easy recipe is a fantastic way to make a quick, delicious breakfast for fruit fans. It's a healthy mix of apple, yogurt and spice, blended to create a drink that tastes like apple pie in a glass.

8 dessert apples, peeled and cored

400g (14oz) natural yogurt

1 teaspoon ground cinnamon, plus extra
   for serving

2 tablespoons honey

2 teaspoons vanilla extract

handful of ice cubes

100ml (3½fl oz) whole milk

Put everything into a jug blender and blitz until smooth.

Pour into tall glasses. Top with an extra sprinkle of cinnamon, if desired.

TIP

• *Smoothies are a delightful way to use up any fruit that threatens to go bad in the fruit bowl. Try this with overripe bananas in place of apples – it's amazing!*

PREP TIME: 30 MINS • COOK TIME: 25 MINS

Curried fish fingers with sweet potato chips

This recipe is great when you start to introduce your family to more exciting foods because it looks familiar but has great new flavours to explore. Sweet potato fries are a great colour and naturally sweet, so will win over younger palates with ease.

For the chips
500g (1lb 2oz) sweet potatoes
1 tablespoon cornflour
1 teaspoon garlic granules
1 teaspoon paprika
1 tablespoon olive oil
pinch of pepper

For the fish fingers
240g (8½oz) skinless cod fillets
50g (1¾oz) plain flour
1 medium free-range egg, lightly beaten
50g (1¾oz) dried breadcrumbs
pinch of pepper
½ tablespoon garlic granules
½ tablespoon ground cumin
2 teaspoons ground turmeric
½ tablespoon ground coriander
oil spray

Preheat the oven to 200°C (400°F), 180°C fan, Gas Mark 6.

Peel the sweet potatoes and cut into chips about 1cm (½in) thick. Put them in a bowl and mix in the cornflour with your hands. Add the garlic granules, paprika and olive oil and mix again, then tip onto a nonstick baking tray in a single layer and sprinkle with pepper.

Bake for 10 minutes, then turn and bake for a further 10–15 minutes until crispy on the outside and soft in the middle.

Meanwhile, slice the cod into 2cm- (¾in-) thick fingers.

Set up 3 bowls: the first containing the flour, the second the egg and the third the breadcrumbs. In a small dish, mix the pepper, garlic granules and spices together, then stir half into the flour and half into the breadcrumbs.

Dip a fish piece into the flour to lightly cover. Shake off the excess, then dip into the egg to coat, then into the breadcrumbs to cover. Repeat with every piece of fish, placing on an oiled baking tray as you go. Spritz all over with oil spray.

Bake for 12–14 minutes until just golden (break one open to check the fish is cooked through). Serve with the chips.

TIPS
- *If your family are keen on spice, try upping the cumin level and adding a little chilli powder for a more pronounced kick.*
- *Once you've got the hang of the crumbing method, you can flavour the crumbs to your liking. How about a lemon and herb crumb for breaded chicken goujons?*

PREP TIME: 10 MINS • COOK TIME: 25 MINS

Chilli bean burgers

These gorgeous veggie burgers are crispy on the outside, spicy, cheesy and slightly gooey on the inside, and conceal bursts of intensely flavourful sun-dried tomatoes. This recipe makes six burgers, so the hungriest pair in the family can double up their portion.

280g (10oz) jar of sun-dried tomatoes
   in oil, drained and chopped
400g (14oz) can of mixed beans, drained
   and rinsed
400g (14oz) can of red kidney beans,
   drained and rinsed
1 large free-range egg
1 teaspoon chilli powder
70g (2½oz) Parmesan cheese, or
   vegetarian alternative, finely grated
50g (1¾oz) dried breadcrumbs
oil spray

To serve
4–6 wholemeal burger buns
100g (3½oz) salad leaves, such as rocket
6 tablespoons hummus, bought or
   homemade (see page 117)
salt and pepper

Preheat the oven to 200°C (400°F), 180°C fan, Gas Mark 6. Spray a baking tray with oil.

In a bowl, mash the sun-dried tomatoes and beans together to a chunky mix, then stir in the egg, chilli powder and a pinch of salt and pepper. Add the cheese and breadcrumbs and stir until evenly combined. Cover and chill for 10–15 minutes.

Divide the burger mixture into 6 and form each into a burger shape. Place on the prepared baking tray, spray well with more oil and bake for 25 minutes until golden and firm.

Serve in warmed burger buns, topped with fresh salad leaves and hummus.

TIP
• *These are a great introduction to spicy heat for young palates, but if you're feeling adventurous, add a finely chopped red chilli to the burger mix for a kick of heat.*

PREP TIME: 30 MINS • COOK TIME: 12 MINS

Rainbow pizza

Most of us, children and adults alike, have favourite pizza toppings that we choose time and again. This vegetable-laden recipe will help you to break out of that rut, with a new flavour experience in every slice. From cabbage to broccoli, sweetcorn to peppers, kids will learn how to enjoy pizza in a whole new way.

For the sauce

400g (14oz) can of chopped tomatoes

10 basil leaves

1 garlic clove, finely chopped

pepper

For the base

300g (10½oz) strong white bread flour, plus extra for dusting

1 teaspoon fast-action dried yeast

1 teaspoon salt

200ml (7fl oz) warm water

For the toppings

150g (5½oz) mozzarella cheese, grated

½ red pepper, finely chopped

½ orange pepper, finely chopped

35g (1¼oz) sweetcorn (drained and rinsed if canned)

35g (1¼oz) Tenderstem broccoli, chopped into small florets

½ small red onion, finely chopped

30g (1oz) red cabbage, shredded

2 tablespoons olive oil

To make the sauce, put the tomatoes, basil, garlic and pepper into a food processor. Blitz until smooth, then set aside.

Put the flour, yeast and salt into a bowl and mix together. Add the warm water and bring together in the bowl with a wooden spoon or by hand. Turn the dough out onto a floured work surface and knead for a few minutes until smooth. Clean the bowl, return the dough to it, cover with a wet tea towel or clingfilm and leave for 1 hour.

Preheat the oven to 200°C (400°F), 180°C fan, Gas Mark 6. Turn the dough out of the bowl and divide into 2 equal parts. Roll each piece out on a floured work surface to a circle about 20cm (8in) in diameter.

Transfer the pizza bases onto nonstick baking sheets. Spread the sauce onto each, then sprinkle over the mozzarella. Score each pizza lightly into 6 equal slices, then top each slice with a different vegetable topping. Drizzle with olive oil, then bake for 12 minutes, or until the crust is golden.

TIP
* *Try switching ingredients by colour; for example, swap orange pepper for gently sautéed carrot, or spinach for broccoli...the possibilities are endless!*

PREP TIME: 15 MINS • COOK TIME: 10 MINS

Chicken and vegetable black noodle stir-fry

In this dish, the flavours are familiar but it's the colour that will surprise at dinnertime, as the black rice noodles really steal the show. You can buy them in some larger supermarkets, but if you can't find them, use other noodles, or even tricolour pasta instead.

For the stir-fry

250g (9oz) black rice noodles

1 tablespoon vegetable oil

200g (7oz) cooked chicken, torn into
    2.5cm (1in) pieces

50g (1¾oz) carrots, thinly sliced

50g (1¾oz) sugar snap peas

50g (1¾oz) Tenderstem broccoli, cut into
    2.5cm (1in) pieces

½ red pepper, deseeded and sliced

50g (1¾oz) baby sweetcorn, halved
    lengthways

2.5cm (1in) piece of fresh root ginger,
    finely chopped

2 garlic cloves, finely chopped

For the sauce

1 teaspoon soy sauce (reduced-salt,
    if available)

1 teaspoon ground coriander

½ teaspoon mild chilli powder

½ teaspoon ground cumin

juice of ½ lemon

1 tablespoon honey

40ml (1½fl oz) water

To serve

2 spring onions, thinly sliced

1 tablespoon sesame seeds

Cook the noodles in a large pan of boiling water for 4–5 minutes, or according to the packet instructions. Drain, rinse in cold water and set aside.

Warm the oil in a large wok over a medium heat. Add the chicken, carrots, sugar snap peas, broccoli, red pepper, baby sweetcorn, ginger and garlic and stir-fry for 5 minutes.

Mix all the sauce ingredients in a bowl, pour over the stir-fry and simmer for 2–3 minutes. Add the noodles and stir until heated through. Serve sprinkled with spring onions and sesame seeds.

TIP

• *Switch up the ingredients to create a new meal every time: add a handful of aromatic coriander, swap chicken for tofu, or use sriracha sauce for sweet heat.*

PREP TIME: 20 MINS • COOK TIME: 40 MINS

Spinach "meatball" pasta bake

Who doesn't love the sight of a bubbling pasta bake being delivered, piping hot and cheesy, to the table? This bake ticks all those boxes, with lip-smacking veggie "meatballs" with a fantastically bite-able texture that will have you all fighting over the last one.

For the sauce

1 tablespoon olive oil

2 garlic cloves, finely chopped

15 basil leaves, finely chopped

2 x 400g (14oz) cans of chopped tomatoes

salt and pepper

For the "meatballs"

1 large carrot (150g / 5½oz), roughly chopped

1 celery stick, roughly chopped

1 onion, roughly chopped

2 garlic cloves, finely chopped

200g (7oz) spinach

4 tablespoons olive oil, plus extra for greasing

100g (3½oz) plain flour, plus extra for dusting

1 teaspoon dried sage

100g (3½oz) Parmesan cheese, or vegetarian alternative, finely grated

To finish

350g (12oz) wholewheat pasta

125g (4½oz) mozzarella cheese, sliced

For the sauce, warm the oil in a pan over a medium heat. Add the garlic and basil and fry for 1 minute until soft and aromatic. Add the tomatoes and a pinch of salt and pepper. Bring to the boil, then simmer for 10 minutes until thickened.

Now make the "meatballs". Pop the carrot, celery, onion and garlic into a food processor and blitz to a coarse paste. Add the spinach and pulse again briefly until the spinach is chopped. Don't over-process, or the mixture will become liquid.

Warm half the olive oil in a frying pan over a medium heat and tip in the vegetable mix. Fry for 5 minutes, until the vegetables have softened. Tip into a bowl, allow to cool until just warm, then stir in the flour, sage, cheese and some salt and pepper. Roll the mixture into about 25 balls. If it feels too wet to handle, pour a little plain flour into a bowl and lightly roll the balls in it.

Warm the remaining olive oil in the pan and fry the balls for 5–8 minutes until golden all over. (You may need to do this in a couple of batches.) Drain on kitchen paper.

Preheat the oven to 200°C (400°F), 180°C fan, Gas Mark 6. Grease a large baking dish with the extra oil. Boil the pasta for 6–8 minutes until still slightly chalky. Drain, then tip into the tomato sauce and mix well.

Tip the pasta into the baking dish, then top with the "meatballs" and mozzarella slices. Bake for 20–25 minutes until the cheese is melted and bubbling.

TIPS

• *These "meatballs" are fab with all sorts of meals and can be frozen after frying. Simply freeze them solid on a tray, then transfer to a freezer bag.*

• *Try flattening the mixture into larger patties to make great-textured veggie burgers.*

PREP TIME: 20 MINS • COOK TIME: 40 MINS

Puy lentil shepherd's pie

Sundays call for something special. I've chatted to hundreds of parents about their ultimate dinner hits, and shepherd's pie came up time and again. This version swaps lamb for protein-rich Puy lentils, which retain their texture better than red lentils. You can use them in all sorts of dishes; they're great for bulking out meaty meals, adding texture to curries and for using in warm salads.

For the lentils

1 tablespoon olive oil, plus extra
    for greasing
1 onion, finely chopped
2 garlic cloves, finely chopped
1 tablespoon mild curry powder
250g (9oz) dried Puy lentils, rinsed
    and drained
2 carrots, finely chopped
400g (14oz) can of chopped tomatoes
1 vegetable stock cube (ideally
    reduced-salt)
500ml (18fl oz) hot water
1 tablespoon gravy granules
    (vegetarian, if you prefer)
100g (3½oz) fresh or frozen peas
salt and pepper

For the mash

750g (1lb 10oz) floury potatoes
    (such as Maris Piper), peeled,
    chopped into 2.5cm (1in) pieces
    and rinsed well
100ml (3½fl oz) whole milk
3 tablespoons chopped chives

Warm the olive oil in a large pan over a medium heat. Add the onion, garlic and curry powder and fry for a few minutes until soft. Add the lentils and carrots and fry for another 1–2 minutes.

Add the tomatoes, stock cube and the hot water. Bring to the boil, then reduce the heat to a simmer for 20 minutes, or until the lentils are just soft (add a splash more water, if needed). Stir in the gravy granules and peas, season to taste, then transfer to an oiled baking dish.

Meanwhile, boil the potatoes in plenty of water for 12–15 minutes until soft. Drain, then tip back into the pan and mash with the milk, chives and a pinch of salt and pepper. Preheat the oven to 200°C (400°F), 180°C fan, Gas Mark 6.

Spoon the mash on top of the lentil mixture, add a final twist of pepper, then bake for 30 minutes until golden. Serve with fresh vegetables or a green salad.

TIP
- *Add minced lamb to the lentil mix if you want, or try roasted butternut squash, or even stir leftover green vegetables into the mash.*

PREP TIME: 10 MINS • COOK TIME: 35 MINS

Breakfast frittata

This frittata offers a blend of classic Mediterranean flavours. It has potatoes for energy, eggs for protein and vegetables to top up the vitamin content...a balanced breakfast in a single pan. What's more, the piquant onions, sweet pepper, juicy tomatoes and earthy spinach bring plenty of texture and flavour.

200g (7oz) new potatoes

6 medium free-range eggs, lightly beaten

½ teaspoon dried mixed herbs

2 tablespoons olive oil

½ red pepper, deseeded and diced

½ onion, finely chopped

100g (3½oz) cherry tomatoes, halved

100g (3½oz) baby spinach, roughly chopped

1½ tablespoons parsley leaves, roughly
    chopped

salt and pepper

Cook the potatoes in plenty of boiling water for 20 minutes, then drain and leave to cool. Cut into 5mm (¼in) slices and pop into a mixing bowl.

Add the eggs, mixed herbs and a pinch of salt and pepper. Stir to combine.

Warm half the oil in a deep nonstick frying pan over a medium heat, then add the red pepper, onion, tomatoes, spinach and a pinch of salt and pepper and fry for 5 minutes until soft. Tip onto a plate.

Preheat the grill to medium. Add the remaining oil to the pan and pour the egg mixture into it. Scatter the vegetables on top. Cook on a low heat for 10 minutes until the base is cooked and the top is beginning to firm up.

Pop under the grill for 2 minutes to finish.

Scatter with the parsley, slice into wedges and serve.

TIP

- *If your children aren't keen on eggs, think about the flavours they love and introduce them to the frittata. For example, if they love curry, add a pinch of cumin to the egg mix. If they're fans of garlic bread, add a spoonful of garlic purée to the frying veg.*

PREP TIME: 30 MINS • COOK TIME: 1 HR

Baked potato with chunky homemade baked beans

Baked potato with beans is a perfect lunch or dinner. But children get used to their favourite brand of canned beans, so might be reluctant to try anything different. These homemade beans should win them over: they are lower in salt and sugar than most store-bought beans...and tastier, too.

For the baked potatoes

4 baking potatoes

1–2 tablespoons olive oil

salt and pepper

For the beans

1 carrot, roughly chopped

1 celery stick, roughly chopped

1 onion, roughly chopped

1 garlic clove, roughly chopped

1 tablespoon olive oil

200ml (7fl oz) hot water

2 teaspoons paprika

2 tablespoons brown sugar

50ml (1¾fl oz) white wine vinegar

1 tablespoon tomato purée

1 vegetable stock cube (ideally reduced-salt)

2 x 400g (14oz) cans of chopped tomatoes

2 x 400g (14oz) cans of haricot beans, drained and rinsed

400g (14oz) can of red kidney beans, drained and rinsed

To serve

4 tablespoons crème fraîche

30g (1oz) chives, finely chopped

Preheat the oven to 200°C (400°F), 180°C fan, Gas Mark 6. Wash the potatoes and prick deeply with a fork several times – this helps steam to escape and ensures they cook evenly. Pat the potatoes dry, then rub with olive oil and season with salt and pepper. Place them on a baking tray and cook for 60–80 minutes until a knife slides into the centre with little resistance.

Now for the beans. Tip the carrot, celery, onion and garlic into a food processor and pulse to a coarse crumb. Warm the olive oil in a large nonstick saucepan over a medium heat, then tip in the blitzed vegetables. Add a pinch of salt and pepper and fry for 5 minutes until soft.

Stir in the hot water along with the paprika, sugar, vinegar, tomato purée, stock cube and canned tomatoes. Bring to the boil and simmer for 15 minutes. Add all the beans and simmer for a further 15 minutes until thick and delicious. Season to taste, then leave over the lowest heat until ready to serve.

Allow the potatoes to cool for a couple of minutes, then transfer to plates and cut almost all the way through lengthways, pushing the sides to plump them up. Spoon the beans over the potatoes, followed by a dollop of crème fraîche and a generous sprinkling of chives.

TIP

• *To get the same convenience as you would from canned beans, simply make a double batch, cool, then spoon into oiled muffin trays and freeze. Once frozen, transfer the portions of beans to a freezer bag to dip into whenever you like.*

PREP TIME: 10 MINS • COOK TIME: 25 MINS

Chilli con carne-stuffed peppers

Chilli con carne is quick, filling and nutritious, and this version shakes up how you serve it – spooned into peppers, topped with cheese and roasted.

1 tablespoon olive oil, plus extra for greasing

20g (¾oz) slightly salted butter

500g (1lb 2oz) lean beef mince (or veggie mince)

1 onion, finely chopped

½ red chilli, deseeded and very finely sliced

2 garlic cloves, finely chopped

½ teaspoon ground cumin

1 teaspoon chilli powder

400g (14oz) can of chopped tomatoes

400g (14oz) can of red kidney beans, drained and rinsed

150ml (5oz) beef stock (ideally reduced-salt)

4–6 green peppers (depending on size)

150g (5½oz) mature Cheddar cheese, grated

To serve

100g (3½oz) crème fraîche

30g (1oz) coriander leaves, roughly torn

Place the olive oil and butter in a frying pan over a medium heat. Add the minced meat or veggie mince, onion and sliced chilli and fry for 5 minutes, breaking up any lumps – the butter will help the mince to brown.

Add the garlic, cumin and chilli powder and fry for 2–3 minutes, then add the tomatoes, beans and stock and cook gently for 10 minutes until a gravy starts to form. Season to taste.

Preheat the oven to 200°C (400°F), 180°C fan, Gas Mark 6. Grease a baking tray with the extra oil. Slice the top off the peppers and scoop out the seeds, aiming to keep the flesh otherwise intact. Place them on the baking tray; I find it works best to use a small tray so that you can pack the peppers in to help them stay upright.

Spoon the chilli into the peppers until it is almost spilling over the sides. Sprinkle the cheese on top and roast in the oven for 15 minutes until the peppers start to brown and the cheese bubbles.

Serve with a dollop of crème fraîche and a scattering of coriander.

TIP

• *Peppers make a wonderful "bowl" for all sorts of dishes. Use them in place of pastry for a different individual quiche, roast them filled with your favourite pasta bake, or pile high with chickpea salad for a packed lunch.*

PREP TIME: 10 MINS • COOK TIME: 20 MINS

Lentil spaghetti bolognese

Swap your standard spag bol for this simple, nutrient-packed dish – low-fat, protein-rich and on the table in 30 minutes. Red lentils take on flavour beautifully, and this dish, with its gently yielding texture, should win over everyone in the family.

2 tablespoons olive oil

1 red onion, finely chopped

2 teaspoons dried sage

250g (9oz) dried red lentils, rinsed and drained

1 small carrot (100g / 3½oz), finely chopped

100g (3½oz) fresh or frozen peas

2 x 400g (14oz) cans of chopped tomatoes

4 tablespoons tomato purée

500ml (18fl oz) hot water

400g (14oz) wholewheat spaghetti

100g (3½oz) Cheddar cheese, grated

salt and pepper

Warm the olive oil in a nonstick pan over a medium heat, then throw in the onion, sage, salt and pepper. Fry gently for 3–4 minutes until soft.

Add the lentils, carrot and peas and fry for another 5 minutes. Stir in the tomatoes, tomato purée and the hot water. Bring to the boil, then reduce the heat to a simmer, cover and leave to cook for 15–20 minutes until the lentils are just soft, but not turning mushy.

Meanwhile, cook the spaghetti according to the packet instructions.

Transfer a ladleful of the pasta cooking water to the bolognese just before you drain the pasta and stir it through to help loosen the mixture.

Serve the pasta and lentils sprinkled with the grated cheese.

TIP
- *Add chilli powder and a can of beans to this lentil mixture for a quick chilli, or ground cumin and plenty of coriander leaves for a speedy dhal.*

PREP TIME: 15 MINS • COOK TIME: 10 MINS

Minty-citrus pesto pasta with edamame

Lots of kids love pesto, but they won't have tried this version before: delicately minty with a kick of garlic and lemon. Pair it with your favourite pasta for a dish that looks familiar but tastes excitingly different.

200g (7oz) fresh or frozen edamame beans
350g (12oz) dried rigatoni
45g (1¾oz) cashews
45g (1¾oz) blanched almonds
2 garlic cloves, roughly chopped
50g (1¾oz) Parmesan cheese, or vegetarian
    alternative, finely grated
75ml (2½fl oz) olive oil, plus extra for drizzling
30g (1oz) mint leaves
juice and finely grated zest of 1 unwaxed lemon
salt and pepper

Boil the edamame beans according to the packet instructions.

Boil the pasta for 8–10 minutes until cooked, but still with bite. This will give you time to prepare the pesto.

Put the cashews, almonds, garlic, cheese, oil and two-thirds of the mint into a food processor and blitz until coarse. Add the lemon juice and zest, a pinch of salt and pepper and a ladleful of hot water taken from the pasta pan and blitz again.

Drain the rigatoni, then return to the pan and stir in the pesto and edamame beans. Serve sprinkled with the remaining mint leaves and drizzle with olive oil.

TIPS
• *Toss in some chicken, if you wish, to add another dimension.*
• *This minty pesto is wonderful with lamb, new potatoes, pork, or spring greens.*
• *To have some pesto on hand for later, freeze a batch in an ice-cube tray for easy portions whenever you need them.*

PREP TIME: 20 MINS • COOK TIME: 15 MINS

Veg-packed beef burgers

From fast-food joints to gourmet restaurants and everything in between, the humble beef burger is extremely popular. This recipe introduces more colour, flavour and texture, but fear not, it's still juicy, satisfying and – most importantly – great to eat.

For the sauce

3 tablespoons mayonnaise

1 tablespoon tomato ketchup

½ teaspoon English mustard

1½ teaspoons paprika

1 gherkin (35g / 1¼oz), finely chopped, plus
    1 teaspoon vinegar from the gherkin jar

For the burgers

1 tablespoon olive oil

2 green peppers, deseeded and finely chopped

1 small head of broccoli, stalk removed, florets
    finely chopped

250g (9oz) Portobello mushrooms, finely
    chopped

250g (9oz) beef mince (20% fat)

1 large free-range egg, lightly beaten

salt and pepper

To serve

4–6 brioche buns

60g (2¼oz) Cheddar cheese, cut into 4 slices

1 small lettuce, shredded

1 beef tomato, thinly sliced

½ red onion, thinly sliced

2 gherkins, thinly sliced

Place a plate and a mixing bowl in the refrigerator for 30 minutes.

For the sauce, mix all the ingredients together in a bowl, then pop into the refrigerator to allow the flavours to mature while you make the burgers.

Warm the olive oil in a heavy-based nonstick frying pan over a medium heat, then gently fry the peppers, broccoli, mushrooms and a pinch of salt and pepper for 5 minutes until soft. Drain if necessary, then tip onto a plate and allow to cool before placing in the refrigerator to chill.

In the chilled mixing bowl, combine the beef and sautéed vegetables. Mix in the egg, then shape the mixture into 6 equal patties with your hands. Place them on the chilled plate and return to the refrigerator for 10 minutes.

Warm a frying pan over a high heat. Place the burgers in the pan (they should sizzle) and cook for about 5 minutes per side.

Slice the buns in half and spoon over the sauce. Place a burger on each, top with the cheese, then pile on the lettuce, tomato, onion and gherkins.

TIP
• *Swap out the vegetables in this mixture for the same amount of chopped cauliflower, sweetcorn, sautéed leeks, beans or roasted squash.*

PREP TIME: 20 MINS • COOK TIME: 35 MINS

Veggie toad-in-the-hole

A fantastic weekend treat that brings a whole lot of vegetables to the party. Remember, the recipes in this phase are all about bringing the unfamiliar into the familiar, so encourage your brood to embrace this tasty break from the norm.

For the veggie sausages
30g (1oz) slightly salted butter
250g (9oz) leeks, halved and finely sliced
2 large free-range eggs, lightly beaten
3 tablespoons whole milk
2 teaspoons English mustard
130g (4½oz) fresh white breadcrumbs
3 tablespoons finely chopped parsley leaves
1 teaspoon finely chopped thyme leaves
100g (3½oz) Caerphilly cheese, finely grated
2 tablespoons vegetable oil
salt and pepper

For the batter
140g (5oz) plain flour
200ml (7fl oz) whole milk
4 medium free-range eggs

Preheat the oven to 220°C (425°F), 200°C fan, Gas Mark 7. Melt the butter in a frying pan over a medium heat, add the leeks and a pinch of salt and pepper and fry gently for 5 minutes until very soft. Tip into a bowl to cool.

Add the eggs, milk and mustard to the cooled leeks and mix well. Add the breadcrumbs, parsley, thyme and Caerphilly and give it a final stir. Form the mixture into 8 sausages with your hands.

Pour the vegetable oil into a 30 x 20cm (12 x 8in) baking tray and arrange the sausages inside. Bake for 10 minutes.

Meanwhile, whisk the flour, milk, eggs and a pinch of salt and pepper in a bowl until the batter is lump-free.

When the sausages have had their 10 minutes in the oven, carefully pour in the batter and return the tray to the oven. Cook for 20 minutes until puffed up and golden, or 25 minutes if you like it crispy. Serve with plenty of your favourite vegetables.

TIPS
- *Make your own breadcrumbs by popping a slice of white bread in a food processor and pulsing a few times.*
- *These sausages are fabulous in place of regular sausages in all sorts of meals.*
- *After baking, the sausages can be frozen and later cooked straight from the freezer at 220°C (425°F), 200°C fan, Gas Mark 7 for 20–30 minutes.*

PHASE 1 REFLECTION JOURNAL

RECIPE	DATE TRIED	SOMETHING YOU LIKED	SOMETHING YOU LIKED LESS	WHAT TO CHANGE NEXT TIME
APPLE PIE SMOOTHIE				
CURRIED FISH FINGERS WITH SWEET POTATO CHIPS				
CHILLI BEAN BURGERS				
RAINBOW PIZZA				
CHICKEN AND VEGETABLE BLACK NOODLE STIR-FRY				
SPINACH "MEATBALL" PASTA BAKE				
PUY LENTIL SHEPHERD'S PIE				

RECIPE	DATE TRIED	SOMETHING YOU LIKED	SOMETHING YOU LIKED LESS	WHAT TO CHANGE NEXT TIME
BREAKFAST FRITTATA				
BAKED POTATO WITH CHUNKY HOMEMADE BAKED BEANS				
CHILLI CON CARNE-STUFFED PEPPERS				
LENTIL SPAGHETTI BOLOGNESE				
MINTY-CITRUS PESTO PASTA WITH EDAMAME				
VEG-PACKED BEEF BURGERS				
VEGGIE TOAD-IN-THE-HOLE				

PHASE 2

Educate

Well done, you've made it to Phase 2!

If you haven't already, take a moment to flick back through your recipe notes from Phase 1 and reflect on your journey so far. Doing so will help you identify any challenges or sticking points early on, as well as highlighting your successes, which should motivate you to keep going.

In Phase 2, we're going to tackle a key form of resistance you might have already encountered: "But whyyy?" "Why do we have to eat healthily? Why can't I just have my favourite meal every day? Why can't we just have fish the way the supermarket makes it?"

And of course we respond, "Because it's not healthy! Because it's important to eat a wide variety of meals! Because I said so!" But as much as we might want to shut down the dreaded "whys", if we really want children to buy into the journey toward truly healthy, varied eating, education is key.

We don't want to force healthy eating upon our children only for them to rebel and seek out a junk diet as soon as they can. We want to equip them with the skills and desire to make healthy choices for a lifetime.

So, Phase 2 is all about education, from helping your children to understand the basic tenets of nutrition, to assisting their explorations in texture, taste and smell, to growing, picking, foraging and preparing.

The activities in this phase are quite hands-on, and some require getting out of the house and perhaps out of your comfort zone, too. But don't worry, you can complete them at your own pace.

ADVENTURES IN FOOD

LEARNING ABOUT TEXTURE, TASTE AND SMELL

The human senses are a marvel of evolution and remarkably sensitive. Under the right conditions, our eyes can detect just a few photons of light and our ears can hear the motion of the air.

What's more, thanks to our noses and tongues, we are able to differentiate between billions, possibly trillions, of unique smells and tastes. The elements that make up any given food are finite, but the combinations and ratios in which they can appear are almost limitless, each sending different combinations of chemical signals to the brain via the nose and tongue. Each one is like a brand new colour – some are similar, some are worlds apart, all are unique.

And our understanding of the science of taste continues to develop. For instance, when I was a child in the 1980s, there were considered to be only four fundamental tastes: sweet, salty, bitter and sour. During my teens a fifth was added: savoury (also called umami).

As I write, "fatty" is making headway to be included in the list, and ten or more others are trying their luck, from piquant (think the heat of hot peppers or the tang of yogurt) to cool (think peppermint), to soapy and even metallic. With so many different flavour dimensions, it's not surprising that the addition of just a single ingredient can radically change a meal.

And the story doesn't end there, as your mind also plays a significant part in how you experience food. Past meals and exposures to a flavour can affect how you feel the next time you try it, while how a dish looks on the plate can also influence our expectations.

TASK 1: SHOPPING CHALLENGE! KIDS TAKE THE LEAD

Walking around a supermarket is a great way to find new inspiration and to spark positive conversations about food. As we whizz up and down the aisles, ticking off items on our shopping lists, we can also take a moment to cast our eyes over the produce we never pick up, the grains we never consider. Even a glance at the ready meals might inspire us to create a new, exciting dish.

And shopping with kids can be even more energizing. Kids are full of questions and a desire to reach out and grab things, to see how they feel, to learn what they are. Embracing that natural curiosity is a great way to make the most of your next shopping trip. Head to the supermarket with the kids and allow them to take the lead. Encourage them to pick things up carefully, hold them, smell them, read the labels, discuss the colour and think about what they might taste like. To keep them motivated, ask each of them to find the list of items in the table opposite.

If you're struggling to make time for an exploratory trip to the supermarket, you could try a similar activity online. With online shopping, the "search" and "favourites" functions, while really handy, steer you toward buying the same items and ingredients again and again. But with the right exploratory mindset and a willingness to look down unfamiliar virtual aisles, online shopping can be a great way to investigate new ingredients and meal ideas from home, especially if you are short on time.

TIP
- *If you're struggling to find some of the food items listed, think pinkish tuna, spiky pineapple, hairy kiwifruits or coconuts, long cassava or runner beans, knobbly dragon fruit or bumpy pickles – the fresh produce and meat aisles will yield the best results.*

LOOK FOR...	CAN YOU FIND IT?
SOMETHING PURPLE	
SOMETHING PINK	
SOMETHING THAT SMELLS SWEET	
SOMETHING THAT SMELLS EARTHY	
SOMETHING YOU'VE NEVER TRIED BEFORE	
SOMETHING SPIKY	
SOMETHING KNOBBLY	
SOMETHING STICKY	
SOMETHING HAIRY	
SOMETHING YOU HAVE TO BOIL	
SOMETHING YOU HAVE TO BAKE	
SOMETHING COLD	
SOMETHING LONG	

TASK 2: DINNERTIME TASTE CHAT

Next time you're all sitting around the table, why not challenge everyone to see how many different types of flavour you can name, then share the knowledge you've learned in this section. Exploring the science of food in this way is an approach that has worked beautifully in maintaining my children's interest in varied meals, providing them with the tools to explore, discover and discuss new flavours.

How many of the flavours listed can you recognize in the meal you're enjoying right now?

THE MEAL WE ARE EATING IS:	
I CAN TASTE:	**I THINK IT'S COMING FROM THE:**
SWEET	
SALTY	
BITTER	
SOUR	
SAVOURY	
SOAPY	*e.g. coriander*
FATTY	
METALLIC	*e.g. red meat*
PIQUANT	
COOL	

TASK 3: REFRIGERATOR RAIDERS!
FOOD TASTING AND COMBINING

Food combining is one of my favourite ways to win over children and adults alike when they're convinced they hate an ingredient (intolerances and allergies excepted, of course). I take sheer delight in serving up a meal and then, after the naysayer has confirmed that they love it, announcing, "It's got gherkins in it!"

The fact is, we are often simply too quick to write off an ingredient when we have had a negative experience with it, but almost anything can be made delicious, and combining flavours is almost always the way to sweep away any pet hates.

To illustrate this, let's grab a few items from the refrigerator, taste them on their own, then taste them again in combination to see how the flavours change, for better or worse.

Here are some notes from my family's experiments; now add your own.

INGREDIENT	TASTING THOUGHTS – ON ITS OWN	COMBINATIONS TRIED	TASTING THOUGHTS – WITH OTHER FLAVOURS
BROCCOLI	Bitter, crunchy	Carrot	The sweetness of the carrot helped to balance the broccoli.
HAZELNUTS	Smooth, warm, fatty	Jam	Surprisingly nice, the different textures were fun
COOKED PASTA	Tasty but bland, quite dry	BBQ sauce	Too overpowering and the sauce is too thin, maybe with some roasted veg?
CORIANDER	Soapy, bitter, grassy	Tomato	The sweetness of the tomato was brought out by the grassy herb.
CAKE	Very sweet, very soft	Cheese	Weird, but not bad; let's try a melted slice on top of some fruit cake...

WHERE OUR FOOD COMES FROM

A carrot in your kitchen is a familiar thing, but what does a carrot look like while it's growing? If you ask your children how some of their favourite foods are grown or made, their answers might surprise you. A 2013 survey by the British Nutrition Foundation showed that one-tenth of the 11–14-year-olds asked didn't know that carrots and potatoes grow in the ground.

The list of surprising facts goes on, from more than one-tenth of 8–11-year-olds thinking pasta comes from an animal, to almost 20 per cent of 5–7-year-olds thinking that fish fingers are made from chicken.

Understanding where the food we eat comes from is so important, and children will love discovering the weird and wonderful origins of their favourite foods. Get stuck in with the following tasks, and see where your adventures in food take you!

TASK 4: THE ONLINE FOOD CHALLENGE

To find out what your children know about the journey their food takes before arriving on their plates, let's head to the refrigerator!

Let them take the lead in discussing how each item might have been grown, produced or processed. Encourage them to investigate clues such as its shape and colour. Does it have leaves or earth on it? Are there signs of where it might have been connected to a branch, or rooted into the ground? If it's in a packet, does it have ingredients or a picture of where it might have come from? Invite your children to jot down or draw how they think different food items look before they are harvested or prepared.

Next, head online to see how close they were to being right. If you're looking for particularly surprising results, try some of the produce included below.

What did we imagine it looks like when growing? What did we discover?

Peanuts	Bananas
Cashews	Cocoa beans
Pineapples	Chickpeas
Pine nuts	Capers
Mushrooms	Cranberries
Rice	Brussels sprouts
Black pepper	

GROWING, PICKING AND FORAGING

Researching online is great, but nothing beats the educational value and enjoyment of getting hands on with food in its natural growing state.

Helping my mum in the greenhouse at a young age is still such a clear, happy memory for me, and my children look forward to "pick your own" season each year with utter glee. So in this section, we're going to look at some simple ways to get your whole family involved with growing, picking and foraging for food.

TASK 5: GROW YOUR OWN WINDOWSILL HERBS

The ultimate growing experience is to plant seeds, watch little shoots appear and eventually have a plant that you can cook with, but for our next activity we're going to take a shortcut.

So that the whole family can quickly begin to experience the pleasure of eating something they've tended to, watered and watched grow at home, we're going to need some supermarket herb pots.

Head to the supermarket and go on the hunt for the healthiest plants you can find. They should look full, perky and healthy. You'll need the following:

Parsley
Mint
Thyme
Basil
Chives
Rosemary
And one other – see what you can spot!

Once you've brought your new plants home, grab a sheet of paper and create a label for each of your herbs, just like the ones below.

Take ownership of one or two plants each. Here are your instructions:

This plant is yours. Head to the library or hop onto the internet, because you will be researching how to care for it.

You will water it, keep a check on it and collect the leaves for recipes when required.

If you really get into caring for your herbs, you can look at repotting them, working to stretch the plant's yield even further.

If your whole plant is used up during your cooking, that's not a sad thing, it's a great triumph. Your plant has fed your family and made everyone's meals even more delicious! Time to buy another one...

This is such a lovely activity to try at any time of year. If your family fall in love with growing, the sky's the limit. Head to your local garden centre for advice on what you'll need to get started with whatever herbs or even vegetables you fancy growing.

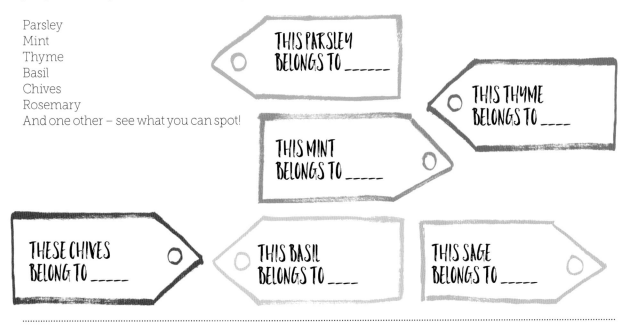

THIS PARSLEY BELONGS TO _____

THIS THYME BELONGS TO ____

THIS MINT BELONGS TO _____

THESE CHIVES BELONG TO _____

THIS BASIL BELONGS TO ____

THIS SAGE BELONGS TO _____

TASK 6: PICK YOUR OWN!

While it's fab to grow food at home, there are plenty of other ways to get hands-on with plants.

This coming weekend, why not plan a family hunt for food? It's a great opportunity to see where food comes from and even to play journalist, interviewing some growers and producers about how the food in their fields finds its way to your plate.

Here are some options, depending on the time of year and what's local to you. Have a look at the meal plans for Phase 2 on page 71 before you set out, as this is a great chance to do some shopping!

- **"Pick your own"** – Depending on the season (usually summer and autumn), find a local grower who opens to the public and pick strawberries, raspberries, apples or plums.

- **Farmers' market** – Visiting a market is a great opportunity to chat to farmers and see produce that is typically a little more leafy, wonky and muddy than the perfect specimens you see in the supermarket.

- **Working farms** – Some are open to the public, so you can see how they raise livestock, and in some cases you can even muck in, helping to feed the animals, collect eggs and more.

- **Foraging** – Find food growing naturally in the wild. It's very exciting but it does require careful research and advice from experts, as it's absolutely crucial that your whole family understands that you must not risk touching or eating anything that isn't safely edible. Look for local foraging groups online that are led by a trustworthy expert who can guide you on a safe trip. If you don't manage to find any, ask your friends if they have herbs or vegetables growing in the garden and, if so, whether you can come and "forage" a few herb stalks or carrots for tea.

Use the table opposite as a prompt to document your adventures as you go.

SOMETIMES CONVENIENCE IS KEY

The recipes featured in this phase reference ingredients you might have gathered on your growing, picking and foraging adventures, but don't be discouraged if you have to buy everything from the supermarket. You've made great strides in investigating where food comes from with your family.

Likewise, don't be nervous to use frozen ingredients if that's what you have access to. Fresh fruit and vegetables are great, but frozen produce is too. It is typically flash-frozen within hours of harvesting, which locks in the nutrients and flavour. A well-stocked freezer can give you access to a variety of veg at a moment's notice, which probably saves me a trip to the supermarket at least once a week. I'm a big advocate of convenience.

INGREDIENT	FOUND IT?	WHERE I FOUND IT	WHAT I LEARNED
CHIVES			
WILD GARLIC			
EGGS			
ROCKET			
CARROT			
ONION			
GARLIC			
CELERY			
POTATOES			
ASPARAGUS			
SUGAR SNAP PEAS			
PURPLE SPROUTING BROCCOLI			
BROCCOLI			
COURGETTE			
BEETROOT			
RADISH			
CAULIFLOWER			

PHASE 2 RECIPES

Phase 2 is as delicious as it is educational.

You're going to experience cooking with the ingredients you've learned about and/or gathered to create peppery and piquant gnocchi, stunning summer rolls, an irresistible fruity oatmeal bake and fantastically fun peanut butter and apple "pizzas".

You're also going to experience messy hands as you delve into spring veg arancini and get kneading to create a stunning chocolate chip braided bread.

Once you've made each recipe, remember to fill in the reflection journal on pages 100–1 to record your family's thoughts.

Let's get started!

Phase 2 meal plans

Here are your two weekly meal plans for Phase 2. Take a glance now and have a flick through to whet your appetite and build your enthusiasm.

As in Phase 1, don't forget to fill in the remaining blanks on the meal plans for yourself. As we've learned, thinking ahead allows you to get creative, to involve the whole family and to introduce meals that make the most of the produce you've gathered and the activities you've completed so far.

WEEK 1

	BREAKFAST	LUNCH	DINNER
MONDAY			HERBY SCONES WITH BLACK OLIVES
TUESDAY	VERY BERRY TOAST		
WEDNESDAY			ROCKET-TOPPED GNOCCHI WITH RED PESTO
THURSDAY			PRETTY DIY SUMMER ROLLS
FRIDAY	PICK-YOUR-OWN FRUIT AND OAT BREAKFAST BAKE		
SATURDAY		TOMATO AND WILD GARLIC FOCACCIA	
SUNDAY		SAVOURY LUNCHBOX MUFFINS	

WEEK 2

	BREAKFAST	LUNCH	DINNER
MONDAY	PEANUT BUTTER AND APPLE "PIZZAS"		
TUESDAY			SPICED CHICKEN AND VEG TAGINE
WEDNESDAY			SPRING VEG AND GARLIC BAKED ARANCINI
THURSDAY			HEALTHIER "FONDUE" WITH VEGETABLES
FRIDAY			FRUIT AND VEG PLATTER
SATURDAY		CHICKPEA BURRITOS	
SUNDAY		CHOCOLATE CHIP CHALLAH	

Herby scones with black olives

Olives might be a new experience for many children and this is the perfect introduction. Their salty bitterness is balanced well by nutty-smoky Gouda and aromatic herbs. The dough takes just minutes to prepare, so you'll be enjoying freshly baked scones in no time.

420g (15oz) self-raising flour, plus extra for dusting
1 teaspoon bicarbonate of soda
100g (3½oz) slightly salted butter, cold and cubed
180g (6oz) Gouda cheese, grated
50g (1¾oz) black olives, roughly chopped
50g (1¾oz) green olives, roughly chopped
2½ tablespoons finely chopped parsley leaves
4 tablespoons finely chopped thyme leaves
200ml (7fl oz) whole milk

Preheat the oven to 220°C (425°F), 200°C fan, Gas Mark 7. Lightly flour a baking tray.

Sift the flour into a bowl with the bicarbonate of soda. Rub the cubed butter into the flour until the mixture resembles crumbs.

With a fork, lightly mix in the cheese, both types of olives, the parsley and thyme. Add the milk and mix again until a light, soft, crumbly dough forms.

Tip the dough onto the prepared baking tray and form into a circle, approximately 20cm (8in) in diameter. Cut into 6 equal pieces, moving them apart on the tray to give them space to rise and spread. Bake for 15–20 minutes until puffed and golden brown.

Allow to cool for 1 minute before placing on a wire rack to cool completely.

TIP
• *These scones are wonderful with an array of chutneys, sauces, dips and spreads. Why not create a tasting discovery plate?*

PREP TIME: 10 MINS • COOK TIME: 10 MINS

Very berry toast

Toast is a go-to breakfast because it's quick and pretty much everyone likes it, but on its own, it isn't particularly nutritious or exciting. However, this wholemeal French toast with fruit compote, yogurt and almonds is guaranteed to jazz-up breakfast time, is super-easy to make and utterly delicious. You can use freshly foraged fruit, but frozen berries also do the trick and save time and fuss on hectic mornings.

For the compote
200g (7oz) mixed berries, fresh or frozen
1 tablespoon honey

For the French toast
1–2 teaspoons slightly salted butter
2 medium free-range eggs
1 teaspoon ground cinnamon
1 teaspoon ground mixed spice
2 tablespoons honey
4 slices of wholemeal bread

To serve
200g (7oz) natural yogurt
1½ tablespoons honey
2 tablespoons flaked almonds

Put the berries and honey into a small saucepan over a very low heat and leave to gently warm through for 10 minutes while you prepare the toast. Stir occasionally, and if it gets too thick, just turn off the heat.

Now make the French toast. Heat half the butter in a nonstick frying pan over a low heat. In a bowl, combine the eggs, cinnamon, mixed spice and honey. Dip each slice of bread into the egg mixture, shake off the excess and place in the frying pan – you will need to fry these in 2 batches. Fry for 1–2 minutes, then flip and fry for 1 more minute. Remove from the pan and cut into triangles. Repeat with the remaining butter and bread.

Top each piece of French toast with a spoonful of yogurt and compote, a drizzle of honey and a sprinkle of flaked almonds.

TIP
• *Try swapping the berries for other seasonal fruits, but cook the compote in the same way. Peaches, apples and plums work well, or how about kiwifruit for a tropical twist?*

Rocket-topped gnocchi with red pesto

If you've been growing or picking rocket during the tasks in this phase, now is the time to celebrate it as the wonderfully peppery garnish to gnocchi. This dish celebrates fresh green leaves – rocket and sweetly perfumed basil. Don't shy away from emphasizing this with the kids: we're eating leaves and we love it!

For the pesto
150g (5½oz) jar of sun-dried tomatoes in oil, drained
1 roasted red pepper from a jar
2 tablespoons olive oil
1 garlic clove, roughly chopped
handful of basil leaves, roughly torn
15g (½oz) Parmesan cheese, or vegetarian alternative, finely grated
30g (1oz) pine nuts
100ml (3½oz) cold water

For the gnocchi
800g (1lb 12oz) gnocchi
1 tablespoon olive oil
20g (¾oz) rocket leaves

Put the sun-dried tomatoes, red pepper, oil, garlic, basil, cheese and pine nuts in a food processor and blitz to a chunky paste. Add the cold water and blitz again.

Tip the gnocchi into a large pan of boiling water and cook for 2 minutes (or until they bob to the surface), then drain thoroughly.

Warm the olive oil in a nonstick frying pan, then tip the gnocchi into it, frying for 5 minutes until they acquire a gentle golden hue. Stir in the red pesto and heat through for a couple of minutes.

Serve in bowls, topped generously with the rocket.

TIP
· *Try swapping the rocket and basil for a more peppery pesto, or use wild garlic or even cavolo nero. You could swap the pine nuts for almonds, or try cashews for a creamy texture. There is no end to the pesto-bilities.*

PREP TIME: 30 MINS

Pretty DIY summer rolls

Here we have a visual treat and a delicious celebration of fresh flavours, all wrapped up in a delicate, translucent rice wrapper that shows off the rainbow of goodies within. Prep all of your fillings first, then get everyone involved in constructing and rolling their own dinner. This is another great way to enjoy homegrown or foraged herbs and veg.

For the fillings

100g (3½oz) thin vermicelli rice noodles, cooked

1 avocado, pitted, peeled and sliced

handful of mint leaves

30g (1oz) peanuts, chopped

juice of 1 lime

1 carrot, cut into matchsticks

1 red onion, halved and finely sliced

½ cucumber, cut into matchsticks

100g (3½oz) cooked prawns

100g (3½oz) firm or extra-firm tofu, cut into matchsticks

For the rolls

12 spring roll wrappers (aka rice pancakes)

oil spray

For the dip

2 tablespoons mayonnaise, or to taste

1 teaspoon sriracha hot chilli sauce, or to taste

Make sure you have prepared all of your filling ingredients first.

Fill a large saucepan with hot water. Immerse 1 wrapper in the water, soak for 10 seconds, then lift onto an oiled board and blot away any excess water with kitchen paper.

Build up your choice of fillings in a line along the centre of your wrapper. Gently fold in the sides, then fold the bottom edge up before rolling upward to complete your summer roll. Repeat with the other 11 wrappers. Everyone can select their own fillings, although young children may need help with the rolling stage.

In a bowl, mix the mayonnaise and sriracha together. Taste and add more of either/both to suit your family's palates. Spoon a little on each plate to enjoy with the rolls.

TIP

- *Fresh salads of all kinds work beautifully in these rolls. Try shredded iceberg lettuce, roughly chopped coriander, thinly sliced beetroot or mushrooms, shredded red cabbage, bean sprouts or anything else you fancy.*

PREP TIME: 10 MINS • COOK TIME: 30 MINS

Pick-your-own fruit and oat breakfast bake

This blend of summer fruit, maple syrup and natural yogurt is baked until set and sliced into breakfast bars with a texture hovering somewhere delightful between porridge and flapjack. It's great hot or cold, and you can throw in the berries from your pick-your-own adventures, too.

450g (1lb) natural yogurt, plus extra for serving

3 medium free-range eggs

1 tablespoon vanilla extract

120ml (4fl oz) maple syrup

2 bananas, mashed

400g (14oz) oats

¼ teaspoon salt

1 tablespoon baking powder

1½ tablespoon ground mixed spice

150g (5½oz) nuts and seeds (such as cashews and sunflower seeds)

150g (5½oz) dried fruit (such as raisins and cranberries)

a little unsalted butter or flavourless oil, for greasing

150g (5½oz) fresh berries (any combination you like)

Preheat the oven to 200°C (400°F), 180°C fan, Gas Mark 6. Butter or oil a 30 x 25cm (12 x 10in) baking tray.

In a large bowl, mix the yogurt, eggs, vanilla, maple syrup and mashed bananas. Add the oats, salt, baking powder, mixed spice, nuts, seeds and dried fruit and mix until well combined.

Fill the prepared tray with the batter and top with the fresh fruit. Cover with foil and bake for 30 minutes, until set all the way through.

Slice into rectangles and enjoy hot or cold, with a generous dollop of natural yogurt.

TIP

• *Use this oatmeal bake to celebrate the fruits of the season and introduce new flavours. Figs work wonderfully well, as do plums. You could also try apples, cinnamon and walnuts in combination for a healthy breakfast "apple pie".*

PREP TIME: 20 MINS • COOK TIME: 20 MINS

Tomato and wild garlic focaccia

Wild garlic is a pungent, tasty plant that is a a joy to forage. If you found some during your explorations, use it here but, if not, chives work just as well. There's not too much active effort involved here aside from some kneading, but you must allow proving time, so it's a great recipe for a lazy weekend.

For the base

7g (¼oz) fast-action dried yeast

300ml (10fl oz) warm water, plus a splash for the yeast

500g (1lb 2oz) strong white bread flour, plus extra for dusting

1 teaspoon sea salt

3 tablespoons olive oil, plus extra for greasing

For the toppings

3 tablespoons very finely chopped wild garlic or chives

4 tablespoons olive oil

50g (1¾oz) Parmesan cheese, or vegetarian alternative, finely grated

2 large tomatoes, sliced

125g (4½oz) mozzarella cheese, drained and finely chopped

TIPS
- *Let the children smell and taste each topping. What happens to the tomato when it is paired with the wild garlic or chives? Does the mozzarella taste different when melted?*
- *Focaccia loves herbs, so try different varieties. Rosemary is a classic, but try sage, bay or thyme, too.*

In a large mixing bowl, mix the yeast with a splash of warm water and leave for 5 minutes – it should bubble a little.

Stir in the remaining warm water, then mix in the flour and salt. Finally, add the olive oil and mix until it comes together as a very sticky dough – don't worry, it will change consistency as you knead it!

Tip the dough onto a well-floured surface, flour your hands generously and knead for 5–10 minutes until smooth. Once ready, it should appear elastic and should shrink back when stretched.

Clean and oil the bowl, then roll the dough into a ball and pop it into the bowl, flipping once to thinly coat in oil all over. Cover with clingfilm and leave to prove somewhere warm for 1 hour, or until doubled in size.

Oil a 30 x 30cm (12 x 12in) high-walled baking tin. Place the dough in it and flatten to fill, making indentations with your fingers for that classic focaccia look. Cover and return to a warm place for another 30 minutes for its second prove.

Preheat the oven to 240°C (475°F), 220°C fan, Gas Mark 9. Mix the wild garlic or chives with the oil, then drizzle half over the focaccia. Press your fingers in again, to make sure you've got plenty of indentations.

Bake for 10 minutes, then top with the Parmesan, tomatoes and mozzarella and bake for a final 10 minutes.

Cool on a wire rack so that the bread doesn't sweat underneath, then slice into strips and serve warm, drizzled with the remaining wild garlic oil.

PREP TIME: 15 MINS • COOK TIME: 20 MINS

Savoury lunchbox muffins

Irresistible muffins, packed with vegetables, cheese, sage and cumin, these are perfect to make at the weekend and then enjoy in packed lunches. If you're following the Phase 2 activities, you can use home-grown sage plucked proudly from your very own herb garden.

2 medium free-range eggs
150ml (5fl oz) whole milk
100ml (3½fl oz) olive oil
120g (4¼oz) Cheddar cheese, grated
2 teaspoons garlic granules
1 teaspoon dried sage or finely chopped
    sage leaves from your herb garden
1 teaspoon ground cumin
250g (9oz) frozen chopped vegetable mix
250g (9oz) self-raising flour
oil spray (if not using muffin cases)
salt and pepper

Preheat the oven to 200°C (400°F), 180°C fan, Gas Mark 6. Beat the eggs in a large bowl. Add the milk and olive oil and beat again. Next, stir in the cheese, garlic granules, sage, cumin and vegetables.

Fold in the flour and some salt and pepper – the mixture will become stodgy, but don't worry!

Line a 12-hole nonstick muffin tray with muffin cases (or lightly spray each muffin hole with oil). Spoon the batter evenly into the muffin cases, making sure each one is level. Bake for 20–25 minutes, until golden on top.

Cool for a few minutes in the tray, then transfer to a wire rack to cool completely. Store the muffins in an airtight container in the refrigerator.

TIP
· *This basic muffin batter works well with almost any vegetables, fresh or frozen, as well as with chopped ham.*

Peanut butter and apple "pizzas"

This "recipe" couldn't be simpler: apple slices topped with peanut butter! Think of it as more of an activity, perfect for allowing children to enjoy getting to know and experiment with new flavours and textures, as well as making the most of freshly picked fruit.

2 tablespoons peanut butter

2 apples, cored and cut into 5mm (¼in) slices

handful of raspberries, halved

2 bananas, thinly sliced

2 tablespoons runny honey

2 tablespoons mixed nuts, seeds or raisins, as desired

Spread a little peanut butter onto one side of each apple ring. Arrange them on a platter or board.

Set out the topping ingredients in small bowls on the table.

Allow everyone to top their own slices, encouraging them to make patterns and faces while experimenting with ingredients they've never tried before.

TIP
- *If the self-topping approach proves to be a hit, try introducing "topping stations" to other mealtimes. A selection of fruit with the morning porridge, perhaps?*

PREP TIME: 10 MINS • COOK TIME: 25 MINS

Spiced chicken and veg tagine

The ras el hanout spice blend used here is aromatic and slightly sweet; enjoy blending the spices and later you'll be able to reflect on how it compares to the Mexican- and Indian-inspired spice blends you'll create later on your journey.

For the ras el hanout
1 teaspoon ground ginger
1 teaspoon ground cumin
1 teaspoon ground coriander
½ teaspoon cayenne pepper
1 tablespoon ground cinnamon
½ teaspoon ground turmeric
½ teaspoon pepper
1 teaspoon salt

For the tagine
2 tablespoons olive oil
1 onion, finely chopped
2 garlic cloves, finely chopped
640g (1lb 7oz) chicken breast, chopped
1 courgette, chopped
2 carrots, chopped
400g (14oz) can of chopped tomatoes
1 tablespoon honey
75g (2¾oz) dried apricots
100ml (3½fl oz) chicken stock (ideally reduced-salt)
fresh coriander, to garnish
juice of 1 lemon

Mix together all the ingredients for the ras el hanout in a bowl.

Put the olive oil in a large nonstick saucepan over a medium heat, then add the onion, garlic, chicken and ras el hanout. Fry for 5 minutes, then add the courgette and carrots and fry for a further 2 minutes.

Add the tomatoes, honey, apricots and stock and bring to the boil. Reduce the heat to a simmer and cook for 15 minutes, until the sauce has reduced and thickened and the chicken is tender. Add a splash more water during cooking if needed.

Ladle into bowls to serve – this is wonderful with couscous, rice or flatbread – and garnish with coriander and a squeeze of lemon juice.

TIPS
- *Did you all enjoy this? Next time, try swapping the chicken for lamb, beef, Quorn, soya chunks or marinated tofu.*
- *You might also like to adjust the spice quantities: up the ginger for warmth; add more cinnamon for sweetness or increase the cayenne for more heat.*

PREP TIME: 15 MINS • COOK TIME: 45 MINS

Spring veg and garlic baked arancini

These scrumptious risotto balls conceal a divine smoked cheese and spring veg centre. Rolling, filling and breading them offers plenty of chances for the kids to get their hands stuck in, so expect sticky fingers and full tummies all round.

For the risotto

2 tablespoons olive oil

3 garlic cloves, finely chopped

4 shallots, finely chopped

250g (9oz) Arborio rice

1 litre (35fl oz) vegetable stock (ideally reduced-salt)

100g (3½oz) Parmesan cheese, or vegetarian alternative, finely grated

salt and pepper

For the fillings

40g (1½oz) smoked cheese, cut into 1cm (½in) pieces

10g (¼oz) asparagus tips, cut into 1cm (½in) pieces

10g (¼oz) sugar snap peas, cut into 1cm (½in) pieces

10g (¼oz) purple-sprouting broccoli, cut into tiny florets

For the coating

50g (1¾oz) plain flour

1 large free-range egg, lightly beaten

70g (2½oz) panko breadcrumbs

oil spray

To make the risotto, warm the oil in a large nonstick pan over a medium heat, then add the garlic, shallots and a pinch of salt and pepper. Fry gently for 2 minutes until beginning to soften. Add the rice, then stir and fry for a further minute until glossy.

Add one-quarter of the stock, bring to the boil and cook gently while stirring. Once most of the liquid has been absorbed, add more stock and continue to stir. Repeat until all the stock has been absorbed and the rice is al dente. The process should take about 20 minutes. Taste to make sure the rice is cooked, adding a splash more water and cooking for longer if necessary. Stir in the cheese, then season to taste. Transfer to a bowl and allow to cool.

Preheat the oven to 200°C (400°F), 180°C fan, Gas Mark 6. Roll the cooled risotto into 20 golf ball-sized balls (using a small ice cream scoop works well).

Take a ball and flatten it in your hand, then place 2 small chunks of smoked cheese and a few pieces of veg in the centre. Wrap the risotto around the cheese and veg and roll into a ball between your palms so that the filling is enclosed.

Prepare 3 bowls, the first containing the flour, the second the egg and the last the breadcrumbs. Roll your risotto balls first in the flour to coat. Next, dip them into the beaten egg, and finally roll them gently in the breadcrumbs until evenly coated.

Place the arancini on a well-oiled baking tray. Spray generously with oil. Bake for 20–25 minutes until golden.

Serve warm – the cheese inside will be oozy and delicious.

TIP
• *Try other surprise centres: pitted olives, chutney or chunks of blue cheese.*

PREP TIME: 5 MINS • COOK TIME: 6 MINS

Healthier "fondue" with vegetables

This isn't as high in fat as classic fondue, but it's just as delectable and offers the perfect way to taste and explore some of the different vegetable flavours and textures gathered during your Phase 2 activities.

For the cheese sauce

500ml (18fl oz) whole milk

30g (1oz) slightly salted butter

1 garlic clove, finely chopped

¼ teaspoon English mustard powder

¼ teaspoon pepper

½ teaspoon nutmeg (ideally freshly grated)

2 tablespoons plain flour

100g (3½oz) mild Cheddar cheese, grated

For dipping

½ loaf of sourdough bread, cubed

small head of broccoli, cut into small florets

1 large carrot, sliced

8 asparagus spears, trimmed

1 small courgette, cubed

handful of radishes, halved

2 boiled beetroot, peeled and cubed

4 gherkins, whole or sliced

Put the milk, butter, garlic, mustard, pepper, nutmeg and flour into a nonstick pan over a medium heat and whisk gently for about 5 minutes until it thickens. Add the cheese and whisk gently for 1 minute until melted and smooth. Allow to cool so that it is safe for children to touch, then pour into a bowl.

Serve with the bread, vegetables and tongs or forks to help with dipping.

If your children are reluctant to try some of the dipping items, how about making it into a sort of game? Everyone tries each item at the same time: 3...2...1...taste!

TIP

• *Take your fondue up a notch by introducing more savoury dipping treats such as cooked meats, marinated tofu or kimchi.*

Fruit and veg platter

There's very little work here – the real skill comes in encouraging your children (and yourself!) to try as many flavours as possible, including those you find challenging. Below is a list of suggested ingredients. Aim for everyone to try at least three tastes they've never tried before.

For the fruit selection
1 thick slice of honeydew melon, peeled and
    cut into small wedges
1 kiwifruit, peeled and quartered
100g (3½oz) pomegranate seeds
2 fresh figs, quartered
2 strawberries, hulled and quartered

For the veg selection
125g (4½oz) cauliflower, cut into small florets
1 carrot, sliced
2 celery sticks, cut into 10cm (4in) batons
70g (2½oz) broccoli, cut into florets
100g (3½oz) baby sweetcorn, sliced
    lengthways
100g (3½oz) mixed nuts and seeds

For the sweet dip
150g (5½oz) natural yogurt
1 teaspoon honey

For the savoury dip
100g (3½oz) crème fraîche
6 tablespoons finely chopped chives
salt and pepper

To serve
hummus

Prepare your fruit and veg and arrange on a large board. Aim to make it as attractive and colourful as possible.

Mix all the ingredients for the dips in 2 bowls. Serve along with a small bowl of hummus and enjoy.

TIP
· *Does your family have as large a competitive streak as mine? If so, to make things interesting, draw up a list of every fruit and veg on the board. Who can tick off the most items tried?*

PREP TIME: 30 MINS • COOK TIME: 20 MINS

Chickpea burritos

You'll find creamy avocado, chilli-flecked brown rice and plenty of leafy greens in this bountiful burrito, and the marinated chickpeas make it as healthy as it is delicious. You can include fresh chives and coriander from your herb growing and foraging challenge here.

For the tortillas
3 tablespoons vegetable oil
75ml (2½fl oz) whole milk
6 tablespoons water
350g (12oz) plain flour
¾ teaspoon baking powder
¼ teaspoon salt

For the rice
250g (9oz) cooked brown rice
1 red chilli, deseeded and finely chopped
1 red onion, finely chopped
handful of coriander, roughly torn
salt and pepper

For the chickpeas
2 x 400g (14oz) cans of chickpeas, drained and rinsed
2 tablespoons tomato purée
1 teaspoon white wine vinegar
1 tablespoon honey
1 garlic clove, finely chopped
1 teaspoon paprika
1 teaspoon ground coriander

To serve
150ml (5fl oz) soured cream
1½ tablespoons finely chopped chives
juice of 1 lime
40g (1½oz) spinach

To make the tortillas, mix the oil and milk with the measured water in a bowl. In another bowl, mix the flour, baking powder and salt. Make a well in the dry ingredients, pour in the wet ones and mix together. Roll into a ball of dough – don't overwork, or it'll make the final result tough – wrap with clingfilm and rest for 30 minutes.

Cut the dough into 6 equal chunks. Roll each into a ball, and then flatten into round tortillas about 25cm (10in) wide. Put a large frying pan over a high heat and, when it's hot, cook each tortilla for just 30 seconds each side – they don't need any longer – so that they have a tiny bit of colour. Wrap all the tortillas in a warm, slightly damp tea towel as you work to keep them soft.

Put the cooked rice in a bowl and add the chilli, onion and coriander. Stir through and season to taste.

Tip the chickpeas into a bowl with all the other ingredients and a pinch of salt and pepper. Mix together, then tip them into a dry frying pan over a medium heat and cook for 5–6 minutes, until heated through.

Mix the soured cream, chives and lime juice in a small bowl and season to taste.

To assemble the burritos, place a tortilla on a plate and spoon one-quarter of the rice in a long line across the middle, followed by one-quarter of the chickpea mix. Top with a few spinach leaves, and a drizzle of soured cream dressing. Tuck in the sides to enclose the filling, then roll up tight to complete your burrito.

TIPS
• *Next time, try flavouring the chickpeas with a minty marinade, lemon juice or cumin.*
• *Why not try these chickpeas stirred into pasta or scattered over salad?*

PREP TIME: 30 MINS • COOK TIME: 30 MINS

Chocolate chip challah

Challah is a braided Jewish loaf, enriched with eggs and honey. Here, the plaited dough is made extra special with a generous handful of dark chocolate chips. It takes some time to prove, form and braid this dough, so it's a perfect weekend activity when you want an afternoon of family time. Enjoy it for lunch with sliced banana for an alternative take on lunchtime sandwiches.

125ml (4fl oz) warm water

2½ teaspoons fast-action dried yeast

1 teaspoon caster sugar

4 large free-range eggs, lightly beaten

75g (2¾oz) honey

80ml (2½fl oz) vegetable oil, plus extra
    for greasing

550g (1lb 4oz) plain flour, plus extra
    for dusting

1 teaspoon salt

100g (3½oz) small dark chocolate chips

In a mixing bowl, combine 75ml (2½fl oz) of the warm water with the yeast and sugar and leave for 10 minutes until frothy.

Mix in the remaining warm water, 3 of the eggs (keep 1 for later), the honey and the oil. Gradually add the flour and salt, mixing until a dough forms.

Tip the dough onto a floured board, kneading until smooth, then knead in the chocolate chips.

Put the dough into a clean, oiled bowl, turning once to coat, then cover with a damp tea towel and leave to prove somewhere warm for 1 hour until doubled in size.

Punch the dough back down, tip onto a floured surface and knead briefly until smooth. Cut the dough into 3 equal pieces and roll each into a sausage shape.

Stretch and roll each length of dough until about 60cm (24in) long, with tapered ends. Braid the 3 lengths of dough just as you would plait a child's hair. I find it easiest to start from the middle, braid to the end, then turn the bread 180° and braid to the other end, tucking in the ends to form a neat loaf.

Grease and line a large baking sheet with baking paper. Carefully transfer the dough to the baking sheet, cover with a clean damp cloth and rest for 45 minutes.

Preheat the oven to 200°C (400°F), 180°C fan, Gas Mark 6. Beat the remaining egg and brush it all over the loaf, then pop it into the oven and bake for 15 minutes. Remove and brush any paler areas where the strands meet with more egg wash. Return to the oven to cook for a further 15 minutes until deep golden brown. To check it's cooked, turn the loaf over and tap the base – it should sound hollow.

TIP

• *Make the challah savoury by adding finely chopped basil leaves and sun-dried tomatoes instead of the dark chocolate chips, or make it sweet with dried apple pieces and ground cinnamon.*

PHASE 2 REFLECTION JOURNAL

RECIPE	DATE TRIED	SOMETHING YOU LIKED	SOMETHING YOU LIKED LESS	WHAT TO CHANGE NEXT TIME
HERBY SCONES WITH BLACK OLIVES				
VERY BERRY TOAST				
ROCKET-TOPPED GNOCCHI WITH RED PESTO				
PRETTY DIY SUMMER ROLLS				
PICK-YOUR-OWN FRUIT AND OAT BREAKFAST BAKE				
TOMATO AND WILD GARLIC FOCACCIA				
SAVOURY LUNCHBOX MUFFINS				

RECIPE	DATE TRIED	SOMETHING YOU LIKED	SOMETHING YOU LIKED LESS	WHAT TO CHANGE NEXT TIME
PEANUT BUTTER AND APPLE "PIZZAS"				
SPICED CHICKEN AND VEG TAGINE				
SPRING VEG AND GARLIC BAKED ARANCINI				
HEALTHIER "FONDUE" WITH VEGETABLES				
FRUIT AND VEG PLATTER				
CHICKPEA BURRITOS				
CHOCOLATE CHIP CHALLAH				

PHASE 3

Discover the fun in food

In Phase 2, we learned how (re)educating yourself and your children on where food comes from and how to prepare and cook it can help the whole family find new joy in eating together.

In Phase 3, we're going to reward all that hard work by focusing on fun! We're going to explore some easy ways to use colour, shape, texture and surprise to bring more adventure to our plates, and we'll also look at how to make family meals into even more of an experience.

There'll be activities to help brighten up your meals, recipes that will see you decorate your plate, and challenges to help you think about how to switch up your daily mealtimes.

THE JOY OF FOOD

THE PRINCIPLES OF FUN FOOD

Food in all its forms is big business, and not just in terms of buying and selling: we humans love to look at food almost as much as we love to eat it.

Online, for example, there's pure delight to be had from simply scrolling through images of beautifully presented food, and we've seen an explosion of internet social platforms where thousands upon thousands of foodie images are posted every hour. People just can't get enough! We seem to adore looking at food that surprises, food that is cute, food that is exciting, food that is silly and food that is creative.

Fun food is often about getting hands-on. We grow up being told not to play with our food, but when what's on the plate looks inspiring, we are always more inclined to eat it; so when it comes to incentivizing children to embrace challenging ingredients, fun is hugely helpful.

Arty plates are a great example, using ingredients to create an edible scene. In fact, we'll be introducing faces and floral displays into our cooking during this phase, in an activity that I've used myself when my children have had friends round; the results have been incredible. Kids who swore they'd never touch veg were tucking in with glee, because they'd made something with it first!

But fun food isn't just for children; it has motivating benefits for the whole family and it can come in many forms. Fun can mean stacking your food precariously high, or dyeing it a crazy colour, using props to serve it or eat it with, combining ingredients in a wildly unusual way, or simply going off-script so far that it wows at the dinner table.

TASK 1: FUN WITH COLOUR

Let's start with colour. Can you design a meal with five different colours in it?

Think about how the ingredients go together and how you could cook or mix them. How would you make sure that all the colours stand out in the finished dish? Why not pop your idea on this week's meal plan?

TASK 2: BOOSTING THE FUN IN AN EVERYDAY MEAL

Now let's try something a little more challenging. Below, jot down a few of your favourite meals, or look back at those you have enjoyed in the previous two phases.

Now, choose one or two of those meals and let's start to think about how we could make them more fun. I've added some examples to get you started. When you're filling in your meal plans for the two weeks ahead, make sure to build in a couple of these ideas. And remember, your notes are always here to come back to if you need further inspiration in the coming weeks.

MY MEAL IS:

HOW COULD I INTRODUCE NEW OR UNUSUAL SHAPES?	*e.g. Try spiralizing instead of grating, or use mini cookie cutters to shape pieces of carrot.*
HOW COULD I NATURALLY CHANGE THE COLOUR TO MAKE IT BRIGHT, VARIED OR UNEXPECTED?	*e.g. Whizz some spinach into a white sauce to make it green!*
HOW COULD I USE DIFFERENT SERVING DISHES, OR DECORATIVE ELEMENTS TO ADD FUN?	*e.g. Invest in some colourful plates, or top with fresh herbs.*
HOW COULD I ARRANGE THE FOOD ON THE PLATE TO ADD FUN?	*e.g. Create child-friendly designs, such as a face, patterns and splashes, or make towers.*

TASK 3: PUTTING THE OCCASION BACK INTO MEALTIMES

Meals are, of course, about much more than just food. They're about the social occasion of getting together, the delight of sharing an experience and the chance to chat and catch up.

When everyone at the table is happy and comfortable, food becomes a joy, not a chore, so what can we do to enhance that experience and create the perfect environment that is conducive to happy, healthy, varied family mealtimes?

Take time to think about how you normally share your meals. Do you all eat at the same time or separately? Are you the type to eat standing at the counter as you tidy up and replenish everyone else's drinks, replace dropped cutlery and generally rush

around? I've been guilty of that... If you all sit at the table, does everyone have a seat they always sit on? Or a job they always do, such as laying the table or clearing away the dishes?

Now look back at your eating habits with fresh eyes. Have you fallen into a bit of a rut? Could you vary things a little?

The amount of space and time you have available will, of course, restrict your options, but small changes are always manageable. You could make a deal with yourself to sit down with everyone at breakfast, or reorganize the seating arrangements, swap preparation jobs, or even eat somewhere else in the house now and then.

Try to add your own ideas to the table below. This will be something you can revisit and add to throughout your journey and beyond, so keep it bookmarked!

MEALTIME	IDEAS TO ADD FUN	I TRIED THIS
BREAKFAST	*Create a "cereal topping station" at breakfast by filling small resealable pots with different fruits, nuts and grains – challenge the family to make fun and playful patterns with the toppings.*	
LUNCH	*Eat outside!*	
DINNER	*Eat breakfast for dinner (and dinner for breakfast).*	

TASK 4: FOOD TO ASSEMBLE

Think of a meal you always serve plated up and ready to eat. How could you break it down into its component parts and allow the family to assemble it themselves at the table?

Fajitas and barbecues are great examples of this, as everyone gets to construct their own meal, so everyone is much more involved and the movement and energy of the meal are naturally enhanced.

Now let's move away from the obvious. Could lasagne be served as separate bowls of cooked pasta sheets, beef sauce and white sauce and constructed on the plate? How about building your own fruit salad? Or composing toppings for your own flatbreads – think olives, feta, rocket and so on – that are then grilled? Suddenly, you're all chefs!

Jot down your own ideas below. It won't necessarily be convenient and you probably won't eat this way at every meal, but as an experiment it is really fun.

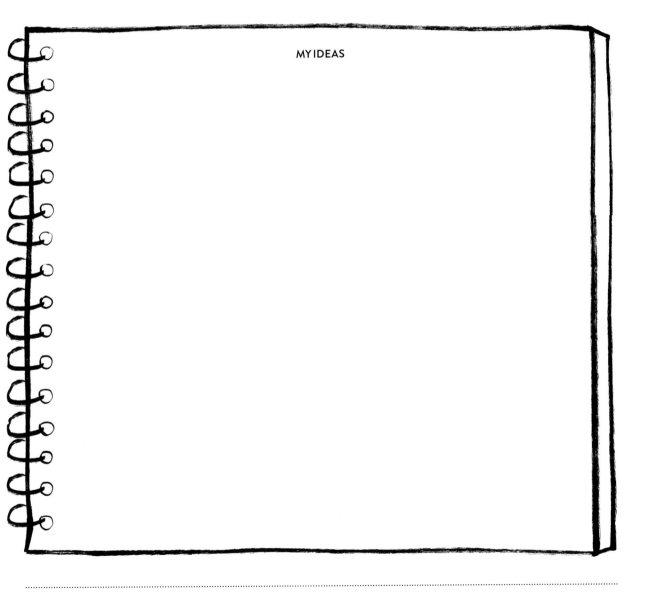

MY IDEAS

PHASE 3 RECIPES

This is my favourite phase because it brings so much joy into mealtimes. You should already be seeing new-found enthusiasm for food, fuelled by fun, and now it's time to have some more!

You're going to get arty with pancake plate art and celebrate colour with a bright red beetroot risotto, rainbow sushi cones and amazing traffic light veggie burger stacks. And you're going to experience new ways of presenting food, with a pineapple smoothie bowl and a "bird's nest" salad. You're also going to play with ingredients in unexpected ways, making tortillas from cauliflower and culturing your own yogurt.

Remember to record your family's thoughts on each recipe in the reflection journal on pages 138–9. It's a great way to reflect on your successes, and to think of new ideas to use when preparing meals in the future.

Phase 3 meal plans

As before, here are your meal plans for the coming two weeks. You'll see there is lots of fun food ahead... and this is your chance to introduce even more.

Using what you've learned about the presentation, preparation and experience of fun food, fill in the blanks opposite. Remember, fun doesn't need to be hard work, but do challenge yourself and the results will be well worth it.

WEEK 1

	BREAKFAST	LUNCH	DINNER
MONDAY	PANCAKE PLATE ART		
TUESDAY			HOMEMADE NOODLE POTS
WEDNESDAY			BRIGHT RED BEETROOT RISOTTO
THURSDAY			VEG-FACE ROAST VEGETABLE HUMMUS BOWL
FRIDAY			TRAFFIC LIGHT VEGGIE BURGER STACKS
SATURDAY		OVEN FAJITAS WITH CAULIFLOWER "TORTILLAS"	
SUNDAY		STICKY-HANDS VEGETABLE SODA BREAD	

WEEK 2

	BREAKFAST	LUNCH	DINNER
MONDAY	SMOOTHIE IN A PINEAPPLE "BOWL"		
TUESDAY			MULTICOLOURED FANCY FINGER SANDWICHES
WEDNESDAY			EASY RAINBOW SUSHI CONES
THURSDAY			COLOURFUL FRUIT AND VEG LOLLIES
FRIDAY	HOME-CULTURED YOGURT WITH FRUIT COMPOTE		
SATURDAY		HEALTHIER CHOCOLATE COOKIES	
SUNDAY		"BIRD'S NEST" SALAD	

PREP TIME: 15 MINS • COOK TIME: 15 MINS

Pancake plate art

We're going to start Phase 3 with creative breakfast plates that are as arty as they are tasty. In this recipe, you'll learn to make a floral scene and an underwater scene, but why stop there? There's some fiddly cutting, so you might want to pre-cut some of the elements for your children, or give them safe scissors to work with.

For the crêpes

150g (5½oz) plain flour

50g (1¾oz) icing sugar

4 medium free-range eggs

270ml (9½fl oz) whole milk

2 teaspoons slightly salted butter

For the toppings

2 green apples

slice of watermelon, cut into thin batons

2–3 mandarins

20 red grapes

a few pomegranate seeds

Sift the flour and icing sugar into a bowl and make a well in the centre. Add the eggs and milk to the well and whisk, gradually drawing in the dry ingredients from the sides to make a batter. Leave to rest for 5 minutes.

Melt a little of the butter in a large frying pan over a medium-high heat. Pour a small ladleful of batter into the pan, just enough to cover the base. Fry for about 1 minute, then loosen the edges with a spatula, flip and fry for another 30 seconds or so until golden brown and speckled on both sides. Repeat for the remaining crêpes.

To make the underwater scene, slice one-third off the side of an apple and place it, skin side up, in the centre of your pancake. Arrange 2 long melon batons to form the stalks of the eyes and 2 shorter batons to form the "arms". Place 4 mandarin segments to form the pincers. Slice 2 grapes into quarters lengthways and arrange them to form the legs. For the eyes, slice a grape thinly and place a disc at the end of each eye stalk. Place 2 pomegranate seeds in the centre of the eyes to complete the scene.

To make the floral scene, slice the edge of the remaining apple thinly to create 4–5 flower stalks and arrange on the pancake. Slice 2–3 grapes into quarters lengthways and arrange in pairs to form the petals of the flowers. If you'd also like to add a bee buzzing around the flowers, place a mandarin segment at the top of the scene to form the body of a bee. Use thin strips of grape to form the stripes, eye and sting. Cut and shape small pieces of apple to form the wings.

TIP

• *Explore the supermarket and encourage your children to look for bright colours and unusual patterns to add to their scenes. This is about creating a positive, enthusiastic relationship with as wide a variety of foods as possible.*

PREP TIME: 10 MINS • COOK TIME: 5 MINS

Homemade noodle pots

Food on the go can be just as exciting as food enjoyed at the table. With these DIY noodle pots, children will build on their growing positive relationship with foods of all shapes and colours as they construct a rainbow of tasty layers.

Vegetables, such as:
carrot, spiralized or grated
spring onion, finely chopped
mangetout, chopped
spring greens, shredded
bok choy, chopped
mushrooms, sliced

Protein, such as:
boiled egg, sliced
cooked meat, shredded
edamame beans
tofu, shredded

Fresh noodles, such as:
udon noodles
glass noodles
ready-to-eat Singapore-style noodles
    (vermicelli noodles flavoured with
    curry powder)

Extra flavourings, such as:
red chilli, finely sliced
lime juice
handful of coriander, roughly chopped
1 stock cube (ideally reduced-salt), crumbled

Prepare your ingredients at the table and encourage everyone to pick at least 1 element from each category so that there are some vegetables, protein, carbohydrates and extra flavours in every noodle jar.

There's really only one other rule when constructing your jars – start with the firmest ingredients at the bottom and the most easily squashed ones nearer the top, finishing with the noodles and your final flavour elements. That way, if you want to take them to work or school, they'll stay at their best.

A great combination to start with is edamame, sliced mushrooms, grated carrot, spring greens, Singapore-style noodles, a squeeze of lime and half a crumbled stock cube.

Pop in the refrigerator to keep fresh. When you're ready to serve, pour in a splash of freshly boiled water (a job for an adult) and stir well. Leave to sit and cool for 5 minutes, then enjoy!

Remember, of course, to be very cautious of hot water around children and wait until it's a suitable temperature before serving.

TIP
- *Adapt this activity for the dinner table, building bowls of noodles using the same principles. Pour in boiling water (safely away from the table), stir well, wait for 5 minutes, then dig in!*

PREP TIME: 5 MINS • COOK TIME: 30 MINS

Bright red beetroot risotto

This is not only delicious, it's also an amazing colour, thanks to a generous helping of beetroot. You might want to wear gloves to grate the beetroot as it's delightfully messy. But you might also rather enjoy dyeing your hands bright red – it washes off, after all!

2 tablespoons olive oil

1 onion, finely chopped

2 garlic cloves, finely chopped

250g (9oz) Arborio rice

1 small fresh beetroot (100g/3½oz), grated

1 litre (35fl oz) vegetable stock (ideally reduced-salt)

200g (7oz) frozen peas

100g (3½oz) sugar snap peas

20g (¾oz) Parmesan cheese, or vegetarian alternative, finely grated

salt and pepper

To serve

2 tablespoons soured cream

handful of parsley leaves, roughly chopped

Warm the oil in a large nonstick pan over a medium heat. Add the onion, garlic and a pinch of salt and pepper, then sweat gently for 5 minutes until soft. Add the rice and fry for a further minute until glossy.

Add the beetroot and one-quarter of the stock and bring to the boil. Reduce the heat to medium and simmer gently, stirring all the time.

Once most of the liquid has been absorbed, add a further ladleful of stock – continuing to stir – and repeat until all the stock has been absorbed and the rice is al dente. The process should take about 20 minutes.

Add the peas and sugar snaps and stir through. Reduce the heat to low, cover and cook for a final 2 minutes to heat the veg. Add the cheese and stir through.

If the risotto is too thick, add a little just-boiled water and stir until you achieve the desired consistency. Season to taste.

Serve in bowls, topped with a swirl of soured cream and a scattering of parsley.

TIP

• *Beetroot is a wonderful, natural source of colour that can be used to turn all sorts of beige foods vibrant red or pink. In small quantities, it doesn't interfere with other flavours. Try grating a little into porridge for some morning colour.*

PREP TIME: 15 MINS • COOK TIME: 45 MINS

Veg-face roast vegetable hummus bowl

Hummus is a big hit with most kids, and this version is packed with flavour thanks to plenty of roasted veg and a glug of honey. But the real adventure begins when you make it smile.

For the roasted veg

½ bulb garlic, cloves separated and crushed slightly in their skins

½ courgette, chopped into 2.5cm (1in) pieces

½ red pepper, chopped into 2.5cm (1in) pieces

2 tablespoons olive oil

salt and pepper

For the hummus

400g (14oz) can of chickpeas, drained and rinsed

juice of ½ lemon

1 tablespoon honey

½ teaspoon smoked paprika

150ml (5fl oz) olive oil

For the faces

30g (1oz) cucumber, halved lengthways, seeds scooped out, then sliced into semicircles

8 cherry tomatoes, halved

1 celery stick, thinly sliced

2 olives, halved

2 carrots, cut into batons

Preheat the oven to 200°C (400°F), 180°C fan, Gas Mark 6. Put the garlic, courgette and red pepper in a roasting dish with a pinch of salt. Drizzle with the olive oil. Roast for about 30 minutes, until the vegetables are just starting to char at the edges.

Squeeze the garlic cloves out of their skins into a food processor. Add the rest of the roasted vegetables, then the chickpeas, lemon juice, honey, smoked paprika and olive oil. Blitz to a smooth paste. If the hummus seems dry, add 1 tablespoon of cold water and blitz again until smooth. Season to taste.

Put the hummus into bowls, and smooth the surface with the back of a spoon.

Use the sliced vegetables to create a range of faces. Can you make them smile? Wink? How about making them look shocked?

Serve with carrot and celery batons as a fabulous afternoon snack.

TIP

• *Hummus is tremendously adaptable: try adding a glug of sweet chilli sauce, or toss in avocado for a guaca-hummus hybrid.*

PREP TIME: 20 MINS • COOK TIME: 15 MINS

Traffic light veggie burger stacks

These look as interesting as they are tasty. Each patty is made with a butter bean base and coloured with a different ingredient – spinach, beetroot, or sweet potato and turmeric. Kids love helping to mould them into patties and, once constructed, this meal is like a traffic light in a bun!

For the base mix
2 x 400g (14oz) cans of butter beans, drained and rinsed
1 red onion (150g/5½oz), finely chopped
4 garlic cloves, finely chopped
1 tablespoon ground cumin
1 tablespoon ground coriander
juice of 1 lime
1 large free-range egg, lightly beaten
oil spray
salt

For the red patties
50g (1¾oz) beetroot, peeled and grated

For the yellow patties
1 teaspoon ground turmeric
50g (1¾oz) sweet potato, peeled and grated

For the green patties
100g (3½oz) spinach, finely chopped

To serve
4 bread rolls
salad of your choice
hummus (bought or homemade, see page 117)

Preheat the oven to 200°C (400F), 180°C fan, Gas Mark 6. Put the butter beans in a bowl and mash really well with your hands. Add the onion, garlic, cumin, coriander, salt and lime juice and mash together with a fork. Add the egg and mix well.

Split the mixture equally between 3 bowls. Into bowl 1, add the beetroot and mix well. Into bowl 2, add the turmeric and sweet potato and mix well. Into bowl 3, add the spinach and mix well.

Oil your hands with a little oil spray and shape your mixtures into patties: you should get 4 of each colour. Transfer to well-oiled nonstick baking sheets, spray generously with oil and bake for 15 minutes until firm.

Serve in bread rolls with plenty of salad and hummus.

TIP
• *Add texture to the burgers with sweetcorn or chopped mushrooms, or give them a little kick with finely chopped chilli.*

PREP TIME: 20 MINS • COOK TIME: 20 MINS

Oven fajitas with cauliflower "tortillas"

These delicious cauliflower tortillas will challenge your family's expectations of what a fajita "should" be. Creating the fajita seasoning provides a great opportunity to talk about the smell, colour and taste of different spices.

For the fajita seasoning
1½ teaspoons mild chilli powder
1 teaspoon ground cumin
½ teaspoon smoked paprika
1 tablespoon garlic granules
½ teaspoon salt

For the tortillas
750g (1lb 10oz) cauliflower florets
2 large free-range eggs

For the sizzling fajita filling
200g (7oz) chicken breast, sliced into strips
1 red onion, sliced
2 red peppers, deseeded and thinly sliced
1 tablespoon olive oil
juice of ½ lime
30g (1oz) fresh coriander, roughly chopped

For the salad
40g (1½oz) red cabbage, thinly sliced
4 vine tomatoes, halved and sliced
2 Romaine lettuce hearts

To serve
4 tablespoons soured cream
150g (5½oz) mild Cheddar cheese, grated (optional)

Mix all the fajita seasoning ingredients in a bowl and set aside.

Preheat the oven to 180°C (350°F), 160°C fan, Gas Mark 4. Line 2 large baking trays with baking paper.

Pop the cauliflower florets into a food processor and blitz until very fine. Spoon the cauliflower into a microwavable bowl and microwave on high for 4 minutes. Scoop it into a clean tea towel over a bowl and bring the corners together, twisting to form a tight bundle. Keep twisting and squeezing to release as much moisture as possible. Get the kids involved – who can squeeze the hardest?

Place the cauliflower in a mixing bowl with the eggs and 1 tablespoon of the fajita seasoning. Mix well until evenly combined.

Divide the mixture into 4 equal mounds and place 2 on each baking tray. Use your hands to form each mound into a disc. Press down firmly all over so that each disc is approximately 2.5mm (⅛in) thick. Bake for 20–25 minutes until firm. Allow to cool to room temperature – each should be flexible, like flour tortillas.

Meanwhile, make the filling. Place the chicken, onion, peppers, remaining seasoning and oil on a large baking tray and toss well to coat. Spread out in a single layer. Bake for 15 minutes until the chicken is golden and cooked through. Transfer to a serving bowl, pour over the lime juice and sprinkle with the coriander.

Toss the cabbage, tomatoes and lettuce together in a bowl to make the salad. Serve everything with plenty of serving spoons and encourage everyone to dig in!

TIP
• *If made in bulk, the fajita seasoning can be used to pep up bolognese, or add a hint of Mexico to mashed potato.*

PREP TIME: 30 MINS • COOK TIME: 60 MINS

Sticky-hands vegetable soda bread

This easy, no-knead, no-prove bread has vibrant flecks of colour thanks to a generous handful of carrot and courgette. Expect to get messy, sticky hands as you make the dough – it's all part of the experience!

50g (1¾oz) carrot, shredded

50g (1¾oz) courgette, shredded

400ml (14fl oz) buttermilk (the thick kind)

1 medium free-range egg

350g (12oz) self-raising wholemeal flour, plus 50–100g (1¾–3½oz) for dusting

1 teaspoon bicarbonate of soda

Preheat the oven to 220°C (400°F), 200°C fan, Gas Mark 6. Line a 500g (1lb) loaf tin with nonstick baking paper.

Grab 2 bowls, and tip all the wet ingredients (carrot, courgette, buttermilk, egg) into one, and the dry ingredients (flour and bicarbonate of soda) into the other. Mix each bowl well.

Form a well in the middle of the dry ingredients, then pour the wet ingredients into it. Mix until well combined.

Dust your work surface with the extra flour and tip the dough onto it. Gently form the dough into a sticky rectangle, just firm enough to hold its shape and place in the prepared tin.

Score some 1cm (½in) deep lines in the top and bake for 50–60 minutes.

To test if the loaf is baked through, take the loaf out of the tin and tap on the bottom to see if it sounds hollow. Leave to cool inside the tin with a clean tea towel over the top (this helps to soften the crust a little).

TIP
• *Try adding nuts and seeds, or experiment with other veg: grated beetroot will turn your loaf pink!*

PREP TIME: 10 MINS

Smoothie in a pineapple "bowl"

To really put some enjoyment into breakfast, this smoothie is served in a hollowed-out pineapple.

1 pineapple
200g (7oz) natural yogurt
100g (3½oz) mixed berries, frozen
1 banana, cut into chunks, frozen the
    night before
3 tablespoons rolled oats
2 sprigs of mint

Cut the pineapple in half lengthways and trim out the core (this bit is usually too woody to eat, so just discard it). Carefully hollow out the rest of the pineapple – take care not to pierce through the outer skin – and cut the removed pineapple flesh into pieces.

Pop the pineapple pieces into a food processor with the yogurt, berries, banana and oats. Whizz until smooth.

Spoon or pour the thick smoothie mixture back into the pineapple halves, top with the leaves from the mint sprigs and enjoy!

TIP
- *Here's a family challenge: what other fruit could you use to serve up a smoothie bowl? Honeydew melon? Oranges? Apples? Get creative and see what you come up with.*

PREP TIME: 15 MINS

Multicoloured fancy finger sandwiches

Sandwiches are an absolutely classic example of a food that people of all ages get stuck in their ways about and, boy, can they get boring! These versions make them super-enticing with brightly coloured layers. Try presenting them as part of an afternoon tea if you're feeling extra fancy.

50g (1¾oz) cream cheese

½ boiled beetroot, finely chopped

8 slices of wholemeal bread

50g (1¾oz) hummus (bought or homemade, see page 117)

1 small carrot, grated

50g (1¾oz) sun-dried tomatoes, finely chopped

30g (1oz) black olives, finely chopped

In a small bowl, mix the cream cheese with the beetroot. Spread onto 2 slices of bread.

In a second bowl, mix the hummus and grated carrot. Spread on to 2 more slices of bread.

In a third bowl, mix the sun-dried tomatoes and olives. Spread on to 2 slices of bread.

Stack the slices of bread up to create 2 sandwiches with a layer of each colour. Top with a final slice of bread (each sandwich will be 4 slices thick).

Using a sharp, serrated knife, trim off the crusts (cook's treat) and then cut 4 finger sandwiches from each stack. Enjoy!

TIP

- *Why not think about more ways to create vibrant layers? Blitzed black olives lend a delightful noir layer. Grated courgette brings a subtle green. Explore the hues of shredded red cabbage or layer up thin strips of yellow pepper. Yum!*

PREP TIME: 30 MINS • COOK TIME: 20 MINS

Easy rainbow sushi cones

Sushi cones – or temaki as they're properly known – are a little less challenging than sushi rolls, so the kids can definitely make their own. I don't claim to be entirely authentic here – I've used smoked salmon to make it easier to source the ingredients in a supermarket – but the result is yummy and that's the important thing.

For the rice
250g (9oz) sushi rice
660ml (22fl oz) cold water
3 tablespoons rice vinegar
2 tablespoons caster sugar
1 teaspoon salt

For the cones and filling
300ml (10fl oz) water
1 tablespoon rice vinegar
4 nori (dried seaweed) sheets
4 teaspoons sesame seeds
40g (1½oz) red cabbage, shredded
60g (2¼oz) yellow pepper, deseeded
    and thinly sliced
60g (2¼oz) cucumber, cut into thin batons
20g (¾oz) pickled beetroot, cut into
    thin batons
60g (2¼oz) smoked salmon, thinly sliced

To serve
1 tablespoon pickled ginger
1 teaspoon wasabi paste
2 tablespoons soy sauce (reduced-salt,
    if available)

For the rice, put the rice in a bowl and wash with cold water. Repeat 3–4 times, then drain through a sieve. Once drained, put the rice into a large, lidded pan with the cold water. Bring to the boil, then reduce the heat to low, pop the lid on and simmer for 10 minutes. Take off the heat and, without removing the lid, leave to stand for a further 25–30 minutes.

Mix the vinegar, sugar and salt together in a bowl. Once the rice is cooked and cooled, fluff with a fork, then gently stir in the vinegar mixture.

For the cones, pour the measured water into a bowl and mix in the rice vinegar. Lay out a nori sheet on a work surface. Dip your hand in the water (to stop the rice sticking to your fingers), then scoop up some of the rice and press it onto half of the nori sheet.

Sprinkle the rice with sesame seeds, then top with a small amount of each filling, concentrating it toward what will be the top of your cone so that it's thicker at the top and you achieve a lovely rainbow look.

Finish by rolling the nori into a cone, starting from the top and tucking in the point and base of the cone. Use a little of the rice – just a grain or so – to stick the edge of the nori into place.

Encourage everyone to try a sliver of pickled ginger, a dab of wasabi and a drizzle of soy sauce with their cones. Remember, though: wasabi is hot, so start with the tiniest dot and go from there.

TIP
• *Try making a sushi bowl, starting with a base of rice, topping with vegetables and fish, and finishing with nori strips and sesame seeds. Perhaps you'll try sushi rolls next?*

PREP TIME: 10 MINS • FREEZE TIME: OVERNIGHT

Colourful fruit and veg lollies

These delicious smoothie lollies contain only natural ingredients and can be whizzed up in minutes. Make sure the kids get involved in adding the spinach and watching the lolly mixture turn green. Remember, this isn't about hiding veg, it's about celebrating all the ways it can be used, and challenging our perceptions while enjoying our food.

4 tablespoons natural yogurt

2 bananas

1 teaspoon vanilla extract

small handful of baby spinach

2 strawberries

granola, to serve

Pop the yogurt, bananas and vanilla into a blender and blitz until very smooth. Pour one-third equally between 6 lolly moulds.

Pour half of the remaining mixture into a bowl. Add the spinach to what is left in the blender jug and blitz again until bright green. Divide the green mixture between the lolly moulds.

Finally, rinse the jug and return the reserved mixture to it. Add the strawberries and blitz until pink.

Pour into the moulds, push in lolly sticks and freeze overnight. Best eaten on a hot day, dipped into granola!

TIPS
- *Cucumber adds a light, fresh taste.*
- *Cauliflower can make chocolate lollies particularly creamy, as can avocado.*
- *Always taste the mixture before pouring into the moulds and add a dash of honey or more sweet fruit if it seems bitter.*
- *Try topping each mould with a spoonful of granola before pushing in the lolly sticks and freezing overnight.*

PREP TIME: 10 MINS • COOK TIME: 20 MINS

Home-cultured yogurt with fruit compote

To make yogurt at home, you need to buy specialist equipment, right? Wrong! It's easy to pick up a small pot of live yogurt from any supermarket. Add milk, gentle heat and a little patience and you'll have a big pot of gorgeous yogurt. This is as much a science experiment as it is a recipe, and will be a great game for the kids. My family will easily eat two big pots of yogurt in a week, so this is a practical and tasty way to make it. You need to start each batch of yogurt a couple of days – or up to a week – before you want to eat it.

For the yogurt
940ml (33fl oz) whole milk
4 tablespoons live natural yogurt, whisked
  to loosen

For the strawberry compote
300g (10½oz) strawberries
2 tablespoons caster sugar
juice of 1 lemon

TIPS
· *Try varying the tanginess by leaving your yogurt to ferment for a little longer next time.*
· *Use a different fruit in the compote – most summer fruits work well, even frozen fruit.*
· *Don't forget, yogurt is also fantastic in savoury cooking. Spoon through tomato pasta for a creamy finish, serve alongside curry with sliced apple, or use as the basis for a lovely tangy salad dressing.*

Pour the milk into a large saucepan and warm over a medium heat until it steams, stirring constantly to avoid scorching it on the bottom of the pan. Turn it off just before it starts to boil (about 95°C/203°F if you're using a thermometer).

Take the pan off the heat and allow the milk to cool until it feels warm but not hot – about 40°C (104°F).

Loosen the yogurt with a little milk from the pan, then stir into the milk. Divide between 2 clean 500ml (18fl oz) jars, put on the lids and place somewhere warm to ferment overnight. The trick is to keep the yogurt warm enough so that the bacteria happily multiply, but not so hot that it kills the cultures.

In the morning, check how firm your yogurt is and give it a taste, but avoid stirring it just yet. If it seems like it needs to thicken further and take on more tang, put the lids back on and leave it for a few more hours. Conventional wisdom suggests anything up to 24 hours before refrigeration is safe.

When your yogurt is ready, give it a good mix to make the consistency smooth and creamy, then pop in it the refrigerator. It will be ready to eat straightaway, or can be kept in the refrigerator for up to a week.

To make the compote, put the strawberries in a small saucepan with the sugar and lemon juice. Cook over a medium heat until the sugar dissolves, then simmer for 2–3 minutes until the strawberries start to darken. Transfer to a clean jar and store in the refrigerator.

Serve the compote dolloped on top of the yogurt for a yummy homemade treat.

PREP TIME: 10 MINS • COOK TIME: 12 MINS

Healthier chocolate cookies

These are easy to make, with plenty of opportunities for the kids to get involved with mashing, measuring and mixing. They may not be quite as sweet as their store-bought cousins, but they offer the satisfying bite and cocoa hit we all love, and they're loads better for you.

2–3 bananas (total peeled weight about
  240g/8¾oz)
3 tablespoons maple syrup
2 tablespoons cocoa
150g (5½oz) rolled oats

Preheat the oven to 200°C (400°F), 180°C fan, Gas Mark 6. Line a baking tray with baking paper.

Mash the bananas in a large bowl, then add the maple syrup and mix well. Stir in the cocoa and oats until evenly combined.

Take level tablespoons of the mixture and roll into balls, then press onto the prepared baking tray. Bake for 12 minutes, then cool on a wire rack.

TIP
· *Add nuts, top with chocolate chips, stir in dried cranberries, or maybe flavour with a dash of orange zest – the choices are endless.*

PREP TIME: 15 MINS • COOK TIME: 5 MINS

"Bird's nest" salad

It takes very little time to whip up this raw veg, lentil, feta and boiled egg salad. And while it's not strictly necessary to serve it in the form of a bird's nest, why not? While the finished dish looks striking, flavour-wise it's about experiencing ingredients in their unfussy form, beautifully combined. There's no complicated dressing to hide the natural sweetness of the carrot or earthiness of the lentils here.

4 large free-range eggs

1 large carrot, either spiralized or shaved lengthways with a vegetable peeler

½ large courgette, either spiralized or shaved lengthways with a vegetable peeler

200g (7oz) cooked Puy lentils

50g (1¾oz) cherry tomatoes, halved

30g (1oz) feta cheese, cut into small cubes

juice of ½ lemon

salt and pepper

Boil the eggs by lowering them gently into boiling water and simmering for 5 minutes for a moist yolk or 7 minutes for a firm yolk. Fish the eggs out of the water with a slotted spoon and place immediately in cold water. Once cool enough to handle, peel and set aside.

Combine the carrot and courgette and pile or twist them onto serving plates to form 4 "nests".

Fill the centre of each nest with the lentils, tomatoes and feta.

Add a squeeze of lemon juice and a pinch of salt and pepper, then sit a halved boiled egg on top of each nest.

TIP
- *What other 3D constructions could you make with food? I'm thinking cauliflower sheep, broccoli trees and more…*

PHASE 3 REFLECTION JOURNAL

RECIPE	DATE TRIED	SOMETHING YOU LIKED	SOMETHING YOU LIKED LESS	WHAT TO CHANGE NEXT TIME
PANCAKE PLATE ART				
HOMEMADE NOODLE POTS				
BRIGHT RED BEETROOT RISOTTO				
VEG-FACE ROAST VEGETABLE HUMMUS BOWL				
TRAFFIC LIGHT VEGGIE BURGER STACKS				
OVEN FAJITAS WITH CAULIFLOWER "TORTILLAS"				
STICKY-HANDS VEGETABLE SODA BREAD				

RECIPE	DATE TRIED	SOMETHING YOU LIKED	SOMETHING YOU LIKED LESS	WHAT TO CHANGE NEXT TIME
SMOOTHIE IN A PINEAPPLE "BOWL"				
MULTICOLOURED FANCY FINGER SANDWICHES				
EASY RAINBOW SUSHI CONES				
COLOURFUL FRUIT AND VEG LOLLIES				
HOME-CULTURED YOGURT WITH FRUIT COMPOTE				
HEALTHIER CHOCOLATE COOKIES				
"BIRD'S NEST" SALAD				

PHASE 4

Step into the unknown

This is going to be a hoot, as we go about cooking up some flavour combinations that will surprise even grown-up palates.

By now, you've already learned so much and come so far, but as a family you're about to push your food boundaries even further.

Get your taste buds ready, because they're in for an exciting ride!

LET'S GET ADVENTUROUS

TASK 1: REFRIGERATOR RAIDERS – THE SEQUEL

Do you remember when we raided the refrigerator back in Phase 2 (see page 65) to taste vegetables such as broccoli and carrot and see how they tasted both alone and in combination?

That was a tentative step into flavour exploration, but this is Phase 4, so now I'm challenging you to call up all your new-found confidence in foodie exploration to try some combinations that are not immediately obvious...or even, perhaps, sensible.

Trust me, my kids absolutely love this activity as it's frankly a bit ridiculous. And I love it because it's a fantastic way to shake off any residual anxieties around unusual foods and make what's coming in the recipes ahead look almost tame in comparison!

So head to the refrigerator and try out some of the most outrageous combinations you can think of. You only need to try a smidge. So as long as it's safe, anything goes.

And who knows, you might even find that some of you love very surprising combinations – after all, some people love banana and mayo sandwiches, and my mum has fond memories of her grandma enjoying kippers and jam! I've included some examples below to get you going.

FOOD 1	FOOD 2	HOW WERE THEY TOGETHER?
BABY SPINACH	DOUBLE CREAM	*Mild and earthy – I might make a dip.*
BOILED EGG	FRUIT YOGURT	*Not good! Fruity and sulphurous do not go well together.*
CHEESE	RASPBERRY JAM	*Actually delicious!*
GHERKINS	PEANUT BUTTER	
TOMATOES	CUSTARD TART	

TASK 2: MORE CRAZY COMBINATIONS!

With our refrigerator experiment safely behind us, it's time to start thinking about what it taught us about our relationship with food. Hopefully, it showed you that you and your family are far, far more fearless than you were a few weeks ago...and it may well have taught you absolutely never to eat fish with chocolate mousse ever, ever again!

Admittedly, you're probably thinking, "That was gross!" but what you've been doing is laying the groundwork to stretch your foodie creativity to new limits, because even an unsuccessful combination of flavours can inspire something amazing that works.

I'm not going to make you do any more wild tasting (at least not yet), but I'd like you to start scribbling down the most ridiculous meal combinations you can think of, the more extreme the better. Tuna sandwiches and

Victoria sponge cake...macaroni cheese and a bowl of cornflakes...garlic bread and strawberry yogurt. You get the idea.

Now of course, if taken very literally, some will simply not work – no one wants prawns and fruit salad – but it might prompt you to think of a brand-new (and potentially delicious) combination such as prawn cocktail with a mango ketchup dressing. You just never know.

To get the most from this activity, you'll need to release your mind from the constraints of the food combinations you know work.

I've added a few examples below to get you started. If there are any combinations that you find utterly bamboozling, make a note and revisit them later. And for those ideas you do think you can make work? Pop them into your meal plan for the weeks ahead.

CRAZY COMBINATION?	WHAT NEW RECIPE IDEAS COULD THIS INSPIRE?
BREAKFAST CEREAL + YOUR FAVOURITE PIZZA TOPPINGS	*Oat base pizza?* *Put the pizza toppings in a pasta bake with a savoury cornflake topping?*
GARLIC BREAD + STRAWBERRY YOGURT	*Garlic bread topped with brie, balsamic strawberries and a herby yogurt dressing?*
TUNA SANDWICHES + VICTORIA SPONGE CAKE	*A giant bread roll, sliced like a cake and filled with layers of tuna mayonnaise and beetroot ketchup.*

PHASE 4 RECIPES

There are few things more exciting to me than discovering new taste sensations, so I am genuinely excited about you and your family trying the recipes in this section.

We're going to be putting fruit into savoury meals with ricotta and pear mini lasagnes, strawberries and cream pasta, and cheese and apple quesadillas.

We're going to be serving up jet black pizza with ackee, experiencing the slimy taste sensation that is curried okra, and wrapping boiled eggs in miso mushrooms to create an incredible twist on Scotch eggs.

And don't forget to fill in the reflection journal at the back of the book so that you can record your family's thoughts.

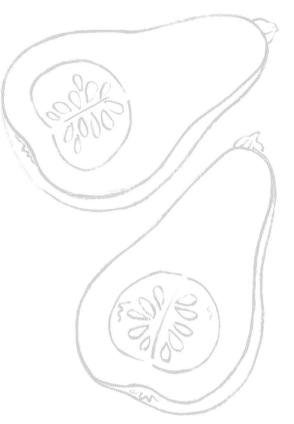

Phase 4 meal plans

Here are your meal plans for the coming two weeks. These don't look like regular family meal plans, do they? Does that fill you with trepidation? Good! That'll make them all the more entertaining...

Don't forget to use what you came up with during this phase's activities to fill in the blanks in your meal plans with more unusual ideas. If you're running low on inspiration, flick back through the recipes from earlier in the book and think about how you could revisit some of them to add a surprising twist.

WEEK 1

	BREAKFAST	LUNCH	DINNER
MONDAY			RICOTTA AND PEAR MINI LASAGNES
TUESDAY			CARROT AND CORIANDER BAKED FRITTERS
WEDNESDAY			BUTTERNUT SQUASH WAFFLES
THURSDAY			STRAWBERRIES AND CREAM PASTA
FRIDAY	PEACH AND PLUM BREAKFAST BAGELS		
SATURDAY		SMOKED CHEESE AND APPLE QUESADILLAS	
SUNDAY		CHUNKY STACKED ONION AND FENNEL BURGERS	

WEEK 2

	BREAKFAST	LUNCH	DINNER
MONDAY			SMASHED AVOCADO ON SEEDED SUN-DRIED TOMATO TOAST
TUESDAY	BANANA-COCOA-PEANUT BUTTER OVERNIGHT OATS		
WEDNESDAY			VEGGIE SCOTCH EGGS
THURSDAY			BLACK CRUST PIZZA WITH ACKEE
FRIDAY			RICE AND BEANS TORTILLA CUPS
SATURDAY		MIDDLE EASTERN-INSPIRED WARM CHICKPEA SALAD	
SUNDAY		OKRA AND LENTIL CURRY	

PREP TIME: 15 MINS • COOK TIME: 10 MINS

Ricotta and pear mini lasagnes

Let's break all the pasta rules with these intriguing mini lasagnes, all about combining ingredients you wouldn't think worked well together. They're quick to make and perfect for lunch.

1 tablespoon olive oil

2 firm pears, peeled, cored and finely chopped

2 garlic cloves, finely chopped

250g (9oz) ricotta cheese, drained

40g (1¾oz) Parmesan cheese, or vegetarian alternative, finely grated

4 tablespoons finely chopped parsley leaves

¼ teaspoon ground nutmeg

4 fresh egg lasagne sheets (170g/6oz)

10g (¼oz) walnuts, roughly chopped

salt and pepper

Warm the oil in a nonstick frying pan over a medium heat. Add the pears and garlic and fry for 4–5 minutes until most of the liquid has evaporated.

Add the ricotta, Parmesan, parsley and nutmeg and stir for 1 minute until warmed through. Turn off the heat and season.

Using an 8cm (3in) cutter, stamp 4 discs from each lasagne sheet (so that you have 16 discs).

Place the lasagne discs in a heatproof bowl, cover with boiling water and let stand for 2–3 minutes until al dente.

Place 2 tablespoons of the filling on each plate and top with a pasta disc. Repeat until you have a pretty tower of pasta, 4 discs high per stack.

Finish with a final spoonful of filling, a scattering of walnuts and a milling of pepper.

TIP
• *What other fillings could you use? Tomato and olive? Carrot and coriander? Parsnip and cumin? They all taste great.*

PREP TIME: 10 MINS • COOK TIME: 20 MINS

Carrot and coriander baked fritters

Carrot and coriander make a winning combination but it's rarely served quite like this. These unusual potato fritters are sure to have everyone coming back for more. They're great as a replacement for hash browns as part of a cooked breakfast, and wonderful for lunch.

250g (9oz) carrot, grated
½ red onion, grated
200g (7oz) potatoes, grated
2 large free-range eggs
40g (1½oz) plain flour
1 garlic clove, finely chopped
handful of fresh coriander
olive oil, for greasing
salt and pepper

Preheat the oven to 220°C (425°F), 200°C fan, Gas Mark 7. Oil a baking tray and place in the oven until hot.

Put the grated carrot, onion and potatoes in a clean tea towel. Twist and squeeze over a bowl until no more liquid comes out. You can throw the liquid away, or decant it into a sealed container to use in a soup later. Put the grated veg in a bowl.

In a separate bowl, mix the eggs with the flour, garlic and a pinch of salt and pepper to make a batter. Don't worry if there are a few lumps.

Pour the egg mixture onto the grated vegetables and mix well. I find a fork works best for this job; just make sure you get right down to the bottom of the bowl so that everything is evenly coated.

Roughly chop the coriander, add to the bowl and mix well again.

Remove the hot oiled baking tray from the oven. Use an ice cream scoop to pick up the fritter batter mixture. Flatten off the top of each scoop and dollop it onto the baking sheet, making sure to leave a gap between each. Repeat to use up all the batter. (You may need to cook these in 2 batches.)

Bake for about 5 minutes until browned underneath, then use a slotted spatula to flip them over. Bake for 2 more minutes until evenly browned on both sides.

Drain on kitchen paper and eat with a crunchy pepper salad.

TIP
• *You can make a big batch of these lovely fritters, then pop them in the freezer on a baking tray to freeze separately. When frozen solid, transfer them to a freezer bag to reheat whenever you fancy.*

PREP TIME: 10 MINS • COOK TIME: 20 MINS

Butternut squash waffles

These have a delightfully gentle orange hue and sweet flavour, and can be enjoyed with savoury or sweet toppings. You will need a waffle iron, but if you don't have one, you could make fluffy butternut pancakes with the same batter instead.

200g (7oz) butternut squash, cut into
    2.5cm (1in) pieces
125g (4½oz) plain flour
125g (4½oz) wholemeal flour
1 tablespoon baking powder
115ml (3¾fl oz) olive oil
450ml (16fl oz) semi-skimmed milk,
    at room temperature
3 medium free-range eggs
oil spray

To serve
2 tablespoons honey
1 orange, cut into thin slices

Put the butternut squash into a pan of cold water. Bring to the boil and simmer for 10–15 minutes until tender. Drain, return to the pan and mash until smooth. Leave to cool completely.

In a bowl, mix the flours and baking powder, then make a well in the centre with a spoon. Add the oil, milk and eggs and whisk to combine in the well before slowly incorporating all the flour.

Whisk in the butternut squash, then leave the batter to rest for 5 minutes.

Spray the waffle iron well with oil, bring up to a medium-high heat, then pour a ladleful of batter into each hole and close the lid. Exact timings will depend on your waffle iron, but the waffles should take 2–3 minutes.

Repeat with the remaining batter. You will get 8 waffles in all, and, if you wish, you can place the cooked waffles on a wire rack and keep them warm in a preheated oven at 160°C (325°F), 140°C fan, Gas Mark 3.

Serve with a spoonful of honey and slices of orange.

TIPS
• For savoury waffles, try topping with wilted spinach and goats' cheese, asparagus and poached egg, or tomatoes and pesto.
• For sweet waffles, toppings could include different chopped fruits, crème fraîche or frozen yogurt.

PREP TIME: 15 MINS • COOK TIME: 30 MINS

Strawberries and cream pasta

Roasted strawberries walk a delightful line between savoury and sweet. You'll be amazed how much the whole family loves them. My daughter, who is suspicious of anything that dares invade her beloved creamy pasta, was so enamoured with this recipe when I first made it that she asked for seconds.

For the balsamic strawberries
300g (10½oz) strawberries, hulled
    and quartered
1 tablespoon balsamic glaze

For the pasta
180g (6oz) butternut squash
300g (10½oz) macaroni
30g (1oz) plain flour
30g (1oz) slightly salted butter
450ml (16fl oz) whole milk
30g (1oz) Parmesan cheese, or vegetarian
    alternative, finely grated
salt and pepper

Preheat the oven to 200°C (400°F), 180°C fan, Gas Mark 6.

Place the strawberries on a baking tray, season well with pepper, then drizzle with balsamic glaze. Stir, then place in the oven for about 15 minutes until the glaze bubbles. Set aside to cool.

Put the butternut squash into a pan of cold water. Bring to the boil and simmer for 10–15 minutes until tender, then drain and set aside to cool.

Meanwhile, cook the macaroni according to the packet instructions, then drain.

Put the flour, butter and milk into a saucepan and place over a medium heat, whisking regularly for 5–10 minutes until thickened, then season.

Tip the squash, Parmesan and white sauce into a food processor and whizz until smooth.

Stir the hot, drained pasta into the sauce. Divide equally between 4 bowls, top with the strawberries and serve.

TIP
- *Try introducing fruit to other mealtimes – perhaps some sliced grapes in a cheese sandwich, or thinly sliced pear in your next cheeseburger?*

PREP TIME: 10 MINS • COOK TIME: 5 MINS

Peach and plum breakfast bagels

These bagels with cool citrus crème fraîche and warm grilled plums and peaches are a decadent weekend breakfast. The combination is delightful and children will love helping to construct the toppings.

300g (10½oz) crème fraîche

3 tablespoons honey

finely grated zest 1 unwaxed lemon

juice of ½ lemon

100g (3½oz) slightly salted butter

2 teaspoons ground cinnamon

4 bagels, halved

4 ripe plums, pitted and sliced

2 ripe peaches, pitted and sliced

leaves from a few mint sprigs

In a bowl, mix the crème fraîche, half the honey, the lemon zest and half the lemon juice together until combined. Cover and place in the refrigerator.

In a large microwavable bowl, melt the butter with the cinnamon and the remaining honey in 10-second bursts in the microwave. Brush the top and bottom of each bagel lightly with the cinnamon butter, reserving the rest in the bowl.

Place the buttered bagels on a hot griddle pan set over a high heat and toast for 20 seconds on each side. Set aside.

Tip the fruit into the remaining cinnamon butter and toss to coat thoroughly. Reduce the heat under the griddle pan to medium, add the fruit and cook for 2 minutes until starting to brown.

Spoon the crème fraîche mixture equally over 4 bagel halves, then top with some of the buttered fruit. Scatter with the mint leaves and drizzle with any of the remaining cinnamon butter. Top with the remaining bagel halves and serve.

TIP

• *These bagels work well with all manner of firm fruit. Try a cinnamon-flavoured crème fraîche with griddled apples, or pears with a stem ginger mascarpone.*

PREP TIME: 15 MINS • COOK TIME: 15 MINS

Smoked cheese and apple quesadillas

Food rules are made to be broken, so we're going way off script here, with a fruity-savoury sandwich. These quesadillas, made with thyme tortillas, win precisely zero points for authenticity, but I love the fusion of classically English flavours with Mexican-inspired delivery.

For the tortillas

240g (8½oz) wholemeal flour, plus extra
    for dusting
½ teaspoon baking powder
¼ teaspoon salt
2 tablespoons oil
4 tablespoons finely chopped thyme leaves
50ml (2fl oz) whole milk
60ml (2¼fl oz) water

For the filling

300g (10½oz) smoked cheese, grated
2 green apples, cored and thinly sliced
salt and pepper

TIP

• *If you're in a hurry, store-bought flour
  tortillas work well too – just sprinkle
  the thyme leaves onto the cheese
  before popping the second tortilla
  into the pan.*

To make the tortillas, mix the flour, baking powder and salt in a bowl. Whisk the oil, thyme and milk in a jug with the measured water. Make a well in the dry ingredients, pour in the contents of the jug and mix together.

Roll the dough into a ball – don't overwork it as that can make it tough.

Cut the dough into 8 equal chunks, then roll each piece out on a floured work surface into a thin, round tortilla about 20cm (8in) in diameter.

Put a heavy-based nonstick frying pan over a high heat and, when hot, cook each tortilla for 30 seconds on each side so that it has just a tiny bit of colour - they don't need any more cooking at this stage. Wrap all the tortillas in a warm, slightly damp tea towel as you work to keep them soft.

Now start on the filling. Reduce the heat under the pan to medium. Place a tortilla in the pan, sprinkle with a scant layer of the cheese, then cover with a layer of sliced apple and season with a small pinch of salt and plenty of pepper. Add another layer of cheese. Top with a second tortilla. This is your first quesadilla.

Fry for 2 minutes until the quesadilla is golden underneath, then flip with a spatula and continue cooking for a further 1 minute until both sides are golden.

Cut into wedges and serve immediately – or keep warm in the oven while you cook the other quesadillas.

PREP TIME: 15 MINS • COOK TIME: 45 MINS

Chunky stacked onion and fennel burger

These are unlike any burgers your family are likely to have tried before. They have a great texture: both fluffy and smooth – thanks to the spiced batter – and crunchy, thanks to the onion and fennel. And, of course, they're delicious.

For the burgers
1 white onion, halved and sliced
1 red onion, halved and sliced
½ fennel bulb, finely sliced
2cm (¾in) piece of fresh root ginger, finely chopped
½ teaspoon ground cumin
1 teaspoon ground coriander
½ teaspoon mild chilli powder
1 tablespoon olive oil
salt and pepper

For the batter
100g (3½oz) plain flour
½ teaspoon bicarbonate of soda
1 teaspoon mild chilli powder
1 teaspoon garlic granules
1 large free-range egg
50ml (2fl oz) cold water
oil spray

To serve
4 seeded buns
salad of your choice
4 tablespoons mango chutney

Preheat the oven to 200°C (400°F), 180°C fan, Gas Mark 6. Spray a large nonstick baking tray with oil.

In a bowl, mix both types of onion, the fennel, ginger, cumin, coriander, chilli and a pinch of salt and pepper.

Warm the oil in a nonstick pan over a medium heat, then tip in the onion mixture and fry for 3–5 minutes until just beginning to soften. Tip onto a plate to cool.

In a large bowl, mix the flour, bicarbonate of soda, chilli powder, garlic granules and a pinch of salt and pepper. Make a well in the centre of the flour mixture, pour in the egg and cold water, then whisk until you have a smooth, thick batter.

Add the cooled onion and fennel to the batter and stir until well coated.

Spoon the mixture onto the prepared tray in 8 equal-sized dollops, leaving enough space between them so that they don't merge. Use 2 trays if you're struggling for space.

Bake in the oven for 10 minutes, then spray all over with oil and return to the oven for a further 10 minutes until golden brown and a little crisp.

Build your stack with 2 burgers for each bun, plenty of salad, and a dollop of mango chutney.

TIPS
- *Try making mini versions of these bhaji-style treats. They make a great lunchbox snack, or a side dish with curry.*
- *How else might you flavour your bhaji burgers next time?*

PREP TIME: 10 MINS • COOK TIME: 10 MINS

Smashed avocado on seeded sun-dried tomato toast

This easy-peasy savoury soda bread requires no proving or kneading. It's made with natural yogurt and enriched with sunflower seeds and sun-dried tomatoes. Chances are, your family has never eaten bread quite like this.

For the loaf

250g (9oz) self-raising wholemeal flour, plus extra for dusting

1 teaspoon bicarbonate of soda

1 medium free-range egg, lightly beaten

400g (14oz) natural yogurt

50g (1¾oz) sun-dried tomatoes, roughly chopped

50g (1¾oz) sunflower seeds

½ tablespoon poppy seeds

salt

To top the toast

2 avocados, pitted, peeled and sliced

2 tablespoons pumpkin seeds

2 tablespoons pomegranate seeds

Preheat the oven to 220°C (425°F), 200°C fan, Gas Mark 7. Line a baking tray with nonstick baking paper.

Combine the flour, bicarbonate of soda and a pinch of salt in a large bowl. Add the egg and yogurt and mix well. Stir in the tomatoes and sunflower seeds.

Tip the dough onto a well-floured work surface. Knead very briefly to form into a round. If it's too sticky, you can add more flour to your board.

Lift the dough onto the prepared tray and sprinkle with the poppy seeds.

Score some 1cm (½in) deep lines in the top of the dough with a sharp knife.

Bake for 20–25 minutes. To test if the loaf is baked through, take the loaf out of the tin and tap it on the bottom to see if it sounds hollow. Leave to cool on a wire rack.

Once cool, cut the loaf into 1cm (½in) slices. Toast 3 slices per person, then mash some avocado onto each slice with a fork and add a sprinkling of pumpkin seeds. Add pomegranate seeds to give a sweet, crunchy kick.

TIPS

- *Try flavouring the avocado with chopped fresh herbs such as coriander or parsley, or spice it up with a pinch of chilli flakes.*
- *Instead of sun-dried tomatoes, add chopped roasted peppers or pitted olives, or make the loaf sweet by swapping in dried fruit instead.*

PREP TIME: 10 MINS

Banana-cocoa-peanut butter overnight oats

Even breakfast needs a regular shake-up, so have a go at making these jars of oats with attractive layers of flavours and textures. Banana and peanut butter is a great combination…your kids are going to love it! Whip this up in minutes the night before and it'll be ready by morning. It's also perfect if you're on the go – just add a spoon.

200g (7oz) rolled oats
400ml (14fl oz) whole milk
1 teaspoon vanilla extract
4 bananas, sliced
2 teaspoons cocoa powder
2 tablespoons peanut butter
2 tablespoons maple syrup

In a bowl, mix the oats, milk and vanilla.

Spoon half the oat mixture equally between 4 clean 250ml (9fl oz) jars. Top each with a sliced banana.

Stir the cocoa, peanut butter and maple syrup into the remaining oats, then spoon into the jars.

Place the lids on the jars and store in the refrigerator overnight.

By morning, the oats will have softened and thickened in the milk and you'll have the most delicious breakfast.

TIP
- *Try a tropical mixture of mango, pineapple and coconut – both dried and fresh work well. Or how about grated carrot and ground mixed spice, or stewed apples and ground cinnamon for an apple pie-flavoured breakfast?*

PREP TIME: 20 MINS • COOK TIME: 25 MINS

Veggie Scotch eggs

Another great way for kids to get their hands into the mixing bowl while challenging assumptions around what any particular food "should" be. These look like regular scotch eggs, but a bite will reveal mushroom "meat" flavoured with super-savoury miso paste. Sure to win over any mushroom-sceptics in your family.

For the Scotch eggs

6 medium free-range eggs

1 tablespoon olive oil

500g (1lb 2oz) button mushrooms, very finely chopped

2 teaspoons white miso paste

30g (1oz) plain flour

30g (1oz) dried breadcrumbs, plus extra if needed

1½ tablespoons finely chopped parsley leaves

To coat

100g (3½oz) plain flour

1 large free-range egg, lightly beaten

100g (3½oz) dried breadcrumbs

oil spray

Boil 4 of the eggs by lowering them gently into boiling water and simmering for 5 minutes for a moist yolk or 7 minutes for a firm yolk. Fish the eggs out of the water with a slotted spoon and place immediately in cold water. Once cool, peel carefully and set aside.

Warm the oil in a nonstick pan over a medium heat. Add the mushrooms and miso and fry for 10 minutes until the moisture has evaporated.

Tip the mushrooms into a bowl to cool. Lightly beat the 2 remaining eggs, add them to the mushrooms, then mix in the flour, breadcrumbs and parsley.

Squeeze the mixture in your hands to make sure it can be easily shaped. If it seems too wet, add another 1 tablespoon of breadcrumbs and mix well. If it seems too dry, add a splash of water.

Take one-quarter of the mushroom mixture and form it into a large flat patty in your hand. Place a peeled boiled egg on top, then wrap the patty around it, rolling gently until the egg is completely enclosed. Repeat with the remaining eggs.

Preheat the oven to 200°C (400°F), 180°C fan, Gas Mark 6. Oil a baking tray.

Now coat the Scotch eggs. Place the flour, beaten egg and breadcrumbs in 3 separate bowls. Roll the eggs first in the flour, then in the beaten egg and finally in the breadcrumbs, aiming to ensure an even coating at each stage.

Place the eggs on the prepared tray, spray generously with oil and bake for 20–25 minutes until lightly browned.

TIP

• *This mushroom mixture also works brilliantly as "burgers" and "sausages". Get experimental with flavourings and use them as a way to shake up dinnertime.*

PREP TIME: 30 MINS • COOK TIME: 12 MINS

Black crust pizza with ackee

I love how much this dish challenges our image of what a pizza should look like. The secret is simply to use some food colouring! To make this extra special, we top it with sweet, smooth ackee fruit, inspired by a family trip to Jamaica. You should be able to find canned ackee in the World section of your local supermarket.

For the sauce

200g (7oz) can of chopped tomatoes

10 basil leaves

1 garlic clove, finely chopped

salt and pepper

For the base

300g (10½oz) strong white bread flour, plus extra for dusting

a few drops of black food colouring

1 teaspoon fast-action dried yeast

1 teaspoon salt

200ml (7fl oz) warm water

oil spray

For the toppings

125g (4½oz) mozzarella cheese, sliced

½ red pepper, finely chopped

½ red onion, finely chopped

80g (2¾oz) canned ackee

1 tablespoon olive oil

Put the tomatoes, basil, garlic and a pinch of salt and pepper into a food processor. Blitz until smooth, then set aside.

Now make the pizza base. In a bowl, combine the flour, black food colouring, yeast and salt, then add the warm water and bring together with a wooden spoon or by hand until you have a delightfully slate-coloured mass.

Turn the dough out onto a floured work surface and knead for 5 minutes until smooth. Clean the bowl and spray it with oil. Pop the dough into it, turning to coat, then cover with clingfilm and leave somewhere warm to prove for 1 hour.

Preheat the oven to 200°C (400°F), 180°C fan, Gas Mark 6.

Turn the dough out onto a freshly floured work surface and divide into 2 equal parts. These will be your 2 pizzas. Roll each piece of dough into a circle about 30cm (12in) wide.

Transfer the pizzas onto baking sheets. Spread the pizza sauce over each one, then dot the mozzarella on top. Add the red pepper, onion and ackee and drizzle all over with the olive oil.

Bake for about 15 minutes, until the cheese bubbles.

TIPS
- *How about adding sweetness with gently sautéed carrot, or swapping the ackee for fried plantain?*
- *For a real taste of the Caribbean, try adding jerk spice to the veg.*

PREP TIME: 15 MINS • COOK TIME: 25 MINS

Rice and beans tortilla cups

Rice and beans always make a simple, satisfying meal packed with protein. These tortilla cups shake up how you'd expect to see your dinner served and they're an easy way to step up your game.

For the tortilla cups
oil spray
12 small, soft tortillas

For the rice
1 tablespoon olive oil
1 onion, finely chopped
1 green pepper, finely chopped
2 garlic cloves, finely chopped
1 teaspoon smoked paprika
½ teaspoon ground cumin
1 teaspoon mild chilli powder
¼ teaspoon salt
¼ teaspoon pepper
200g (7oz) brown rice
500ml (18fl oz) vegetable stock
1 tablespoon tomato purée
400g (14oz) can of black beans,
    drained and rinsed
200g (7oz) fresh or frozen sweetcorn

To serve
115g (4oz) Cheddar cheese, grated
1 avocado, pitted, peeled and thinly sliced
4 tablespoons soured cream
handful of coriander leaves, roughly chopped

Preheat the oven to 200°C (400°F), 180°C fan, Gas Mark 6. Oil a 12-hole muffin tray.

Push the tortillas into the prepared tray to form cups, folding as necessary and pressing firmly. If you find that they keep popping out, put a little square of baking paper into each and weigh it down with a few baking beans.

Bake for 10 minutes until lightly golden, keeping an eye on them so that they don't burn. Transfer to a wire rack to cool.

Meanwhile, warm the oil in a pan over a medium heat. Add the onion, green pepper and garlic and fry for 2–3 minutes until just softened. Add the paprika, cumin, chilli powder, salt and pepper and fry for a further minute until you smell the aroma of the spices.

Add the rice and fry for 2 minutes, stirring until glossy. Add the stock, tomato purée, black beans and sweetcorn, stir and bring to a simmer. Pop the lid on the pan and cook for 20 minutes until the liquid has been absorbed and the rice can be fluffed with a fork.

Spoon the cooked rice into the tortilla cups. Top with a pinch of cheese, a slice of avocado, a dollop of soured cream and a sprinkling of coriander.

Alternatively, bring the rice and tortilla cups separately to the table along with the finishing touches and let everyone construct their own!

TIP
- *Tortilla cups work to serve both savoury and sweet dishes, so if you're ever struggling to build your family's enthusiasm for certain foods, these cups could prove useful in piquing their interest.*

PREP TIME: 5 MINS • COOK TIME: 25 MINS

Middle Eastern-inspired warm chickpea salad

Salad can be so much more than lettuce, tomatoes and cucumber tossed in a bit of dressing. This version has warm spiced chickpeas, comforting bulgur wheat and the perfume of parsley and mint, finished with salty, creamy feta. Let's turn salad on its head.

100g (3½oz) bulgur wheat, rinsed and drained
500ml (18fl oz) cold water
400g (14oz) can of chickpeas, drained and rinsed
1 teaspoon ground cumin
1 teaspoon ground coriander
1 teaspoon smoked paprika
1 tablespoon tomato ketchup
2 tablespoons olive oil
1 red onion, finely chopped
3 tablespoons finely chopped parsley leaves
3 tablespoons finely chopped mint leaves
200g (7oz) tomatoes, deseeded and finely chopped
juice of 1 lime
50g (1¾oz) feta cheese
salt and pepper

Place the bulgur wheat in a saucepan with the cold water. Bring to the boil and cover, then reduce the heat and simmer for 15 minutes until cooked, or until the water is absorbed. Drain if necessary, then transfer to a large bowl.

In a separate bowl, mix the chickpeas, ground cumin and coriander, smoked paprika, ketchup, a pinch of salt and pepper and 1 tablespoon of the olive oil.

Warm the remaining 1 tablespoon oil in a nonstick frying pan over a medium heat, then tip in the chickpea mixture. Fry for 5–8 minutes until the chickpeas take on a deep golden colour, but do not burn, then tip into the bowl with the cooked bulgur wheat.

Add the red onion, parsley, mint, tomatoes and lime juice and stir through.

Season to taste, dish up into 4 bowls and crumble the feta on top to serve.

TIPS
- This salad is great with leftover roast chicken, beef or lamb.
- Experiment with different grains and pulses. Try adding quinoa or brown rice instead of bulgur, and using kidney beans – or even edamame – in place of chickpeas.

PREP TIME: 15 MINS • COOK TIME: 30 MINS

Okra and lentil curry

Okra is quite an unusual vegetable, with a distinctive look and a unique texture. In fact, it's technically a fruit; the edible seed pods of a luscious green plant that thrives in warm climates. But an unfamiliar look in food is just what we're looking for in Phase 4, so let's get this curry started.

100g (3½oz) dried red lentils, well rinsed

200g (7oz) dried Puy lentils, well rinsed

400g (14oz) can of coconut milk

500ml (18fl oz) vegetable stock

½ teaspoon ground turmeric

2 onions, finely chopped

½ teaspoon mustard seeds

½ teaspoon cumin seeds

2 tablespoons vegetable oil

4 garlic cloves, thinly sliced

400g (14oz) fresh or frozen okra, sliced into 1.5cm (⅝in) pieces

10 curry leaves

½ teaspoon chilli flakes

2 medium tomatoes, finely chopped

salt and pepper

Put the red lentils, Puy lentils, coconut milk, stock, turmeric and half the sliced onions into a large nonstick saucepan and place it over a medium heat. Bring to the boil, then reduce the heat and simmer for 15–20 minutes, stirring occasionally. Keep an eye on the mixture while it simmers as you might need to add a splash of water if it starts to dry out.

Meanwhile, put a dry frying pan over a high heat, add the mustard and cumin seeds and wait for them to start popping – it should take only 60 seconds or so.

Reduce the heat to medium, add the oil to warm through, then add the garlic and fry very briefly until it starts to turn golden (try not to burn it or it will taste bitter).

Add the remaining onion, the okra, curry leaves and chilli flakes and fry for 8–10 minutes until the okra is tender.

When your lentils are almost cooked, tip in the contents of the frying pan, add the tomatoes and mix well. Simmer for a final 5 minutes, then season to taste, spoon into bowls and serve.

TIP

· *I introduced okra here quite deliberately as a challenging ingredient – now it's over to you to push the boundaries. Have you ever made a melon curry, for example? Or a radish curry?*

PHASE 4 REFLECTION JOURNAL

RECIPE	DATE TRIED	SOMETHING YOU LIKED	SOMETHING YOU LIKED LESS	WHAT TO CHANGE NEXT TIME
RICOTTA AND PEAR MINI LASAGNES				
CARROT AND CORIANDER BAKED FRITTERS				
BUTTERNUT SQUASH WAFFLES				
STRAWBERRIES AND CREAM PASTA				
PEACH AND PLUM BREAKFAST BAGELS				
SMOKED CHEESE AND APPLE QUESADILLAS				
CHUNKY STACKED ONION AND FENNEL BURGERS				

RECIPE	DATE TRIED	SOMETHING YOU LIKED	SOMETHING YOU LIKED LESS	WHAT TO CHANGE NEXT TIME
SMASHED AVOCADO ON SEEDED SUN-DRIED TOMATO TOAST				
BANANA-COCOA-PEANUT BUTTER OVERNIGHT OATS				
VEGGIE SCOTCH EGGS				
BLACK CRUST PIZZA WITH ACKEE				
RICE AND BEANS TORTILLA CUPS				
MIDDLE EASTERN-INSPIRED WARM CHICKPEA SALAD				
OKRA AND LENTIL CURRY				

PHASE 5

Cement variety

Congratulations! You've reached the final phase and you're about to cook the final 14 recipes. But, as you know, the purpose of this book isn't simply to arm you with recipes, it's to change your family's eating habits for good.

It's now time to set yourself up with a toolkit for becoming your own recipe creator.

We've come a long way over the past few weeks. We've turned classic dinners into something new and exciting, we've got to know our food and where it comes from, we've had fun with colour, shape and texture, we've broken free from our deeply ingrained food norms, and we've had weeks and weeks of great mealtime variety.

I know from personal experience and from chatting to hundreds of other parents that if you were to stop here, you would very probably continue your creative journey for a time, but would eventually settle on the handful of recipes you like best and relax into a routine where they feature time and again without much variation. Eventually, you might find that introducing new flavours, textures, serving styles and ingredients is slowly but surely becoming a challenge once more. So how do we avoid slipping backward? How can we cement and maintain all that we've achieved?

HABITUALIZING VARIETY: COMING FULL CIRCLE

Phase 5 is all about arming you with the final tools you'll need to become your own best recipe creator, to make every meal an adventure, a delightful experiment in cooking with delicious results. You can achieve incredible things, I guarantee it.

Have a flick through Phase 5 now and you'll see that the recipes take a slightly different turn, representing as they do 14 common foods, from bread, eggs and grains to leftover meat.

This phase contains guidance on how to think creatively around each type of food, and alongside each recipe you'll find 10 further ideas about how to cook and serve it. All in all, Phase 5 adds up to over 150 more dish suggestions for you to start designing and creating for yourselves.

Alongside everything you've already learned, Phase 5 provides enough inspiration to help you maintain creative variety at mealtimes for years to come.

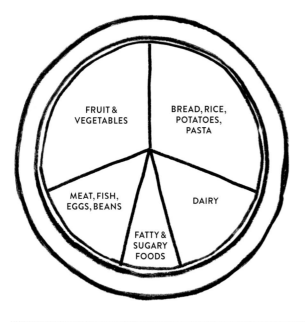

TASK 1: REVISITING CREATIVE THINKING AROUND FOOD

Remember the balanced plate we explored in Phase 1 (see below)? Five core elements, five main types of food to choose from, one dish to make. As we know, we tend to stick with the familiar when we cook, but by breaking things down and building back up again, we're able to go much, much further.

DECONSTRUCTING AND RECONSTRUCTING THE HUMBLE SALAD

FRUITS AND VEGETABLES

Veg (and fruit) are, of course, the core element of most salads. They bring vitamins, juiciness and flavour.

And they bring *volume*. I can think of no other meal that can be served in positively huge bowls and devoured without so much as a stomach ache. That's because fruits and vegetables have a high water content and a typically low calorie density, which is also, of course, why we tend to think of salad as healthy.

The danger comes when salad is presented purely to act as bulk, or as a slightly resented "healthy meal", with little attention given to the flavour and texture.

Salads can and should be joyous meals. Look in your refrigerator, search beyond the obvious lettuce, tomatoes and cucumber. What else could go in a salad?

Courgettes in large uncooked chunks can be spongy, but work beautifully in salad if grated or spiralized – they eagerly drink up zingy dressings. Likewise, you might dislike raw mushrooms, but when thinly sliced in a herby or creamy dressing, they are quite special.

Think about cutting vegetables in different ways. Carrot batons are great with dips, but when grated, their surface area increases and they can bring real sweetness to a salad. Pickled beetroot is mild and vinegary – perfect for balancing sweet salads – while raw grated beetroot brings an earthiness that highlights salty, tangy flavours, such as goats' cheese or feta cheese.

It is difficult to go wrong when thinking about vegetables to put in your salad. Simply taste as you go, enjoy the balance of flavours and take risks.

Fruits can be trickier, but all manner are welcome. Melon already walks the savoury-sweet line, most berries are mildly sweet-tart enough to work in simple salads, dried fruit can add chewiness, while grated apples and pears are great when mixed with sweeter grated roots such as beetroot or parsnip. High in fat, avocado and its buttery, delicate flavour can bring such creaminess to a salad that you can almost do without dressing. Once you've tried everything raw, try them cooked, pickled, fermented and dried!

And don't forget herbs. Basil pairs well with tomato, of course, but there's so much more flavour to discover. Try mint with melon, thyme with apple, sage with squash and so on. Get experimental.

PROTEIN

Now it's time to think about protein. Cooked meats bring texture and umami flavours to your salad and help make it more filling. Chicken, ham, beef and meat alternatives can work well.

Think about flavours that work well together in other dishes. For example, pork is great with apple sauce and potato, so if your salad is packed with earthy vegetables and grated apples, pork is an obvious choice.

Beans are also packed with protein, so can help make a salad more satisfying, as well as bringing a unique texture. Canned beans are typically quite soft, so think about using them to balance out an otherwise crunchy salad. Conversely, edamame beans or chickpeas are quite firm and can lend bite to a grain-based salad.

Eggs bring further benefits to the salad party, depending on how they're cooked. A soft-boiled egg on top of a warm salad brings its own dressing in the form of the creamy, runny yolk, while a sliced hard-boiled egg stands up better in a leafy, crunchy salad.

And finally, I could wax lyrical about nuts and seeds. I cannot recommend highly enough that you keep a variety in your cupboard and get to know their different flavours and textures. Cashews are creamy and mild, almonds are crunchy and perfumed, walnuts are firm and ever-so-slightly bitter. They can lift a salad from predictable and boring to scraping-up-every-last-kernel delicious. Don't miss out.

CARBOHYDRATES

If a salad is made up mostly of veg – particularly if it's also low in protein – it can seem unsatisfying, so the most obvious option is to reach for the bread. That's certainly a valid choice, as bread can be the perfect companion, but there are plenty of other options. In the interests of variety and keeping the norm at bay, it's a good idea to get to know the alternatives.

Warm grain salads, such as the one we made in Phase 4 (see page 171) are endlessly adaptable and remind us that a salad needn't be a cold side dish. Explore wild rice, pearl barley, millet, pseudo grains such as quinoa... walk down the grains aisle of your supermarket and don't leave without picking up something new.

Potatoes and pasta are also great salad additions, and they needn't be limited to the classic boiled new potatoes or mayo pasta. Potato wedges can add warmth and crunch, for example, while tortellini can turn a snack salad into a full meal.

DAIRY

As a rule of thumb, think of this group of foods as the garnish or seasoning to your salad. Dairy can easily overpower but, used in moderation, can be divine.

Smoked cheese can bring a more rounded flavour to a salad, while blue cheese can offer aroma and tang. Salty cheeses, such as Parmesan or feta, can be used as seasoning and to balance out sweetness, while giving grittiness or creaminess respectively.

Yogurt, crème fraîche and soured cream can all make a wonderful basis for a dressing. Try adding a little citrus and spice and see where it takes you.

FATTY AND SUGARY FOOD

Fats and sugar aren't additions you'd immediately associate with a salad, and in many cases they're unnecessary, but sometimes the right fatty or sweet element can turn a salad from good to great.

For instance, where a salad boasts peppery rocket or bitter endive, a honeyed dressing can quickly and simply balance the dish, while letting the vegetables' natural flavours shine through.

Who would have thought there was so much to a salad, eh?

TASK 2: DESIGN YOUR OWN SALADS

Now design four salads of your own. There are only two rules: you must use at least four of the five wedges in the diagram, and you must create salads you've never eaten before.

You'll probably have noticed by now that in thinking about the nutritional groups that make up a salad, we were also able to explore other key elements that make up a great meal, such as texture, flavour, herbs and spices, sweetness and acidity.

During Phase 5 and beyond, you can use the following prompts to help you think holistically – that is, about the whole dish and how its components will work together – when designing a meal.

PROMPT	THOUGHTS
FOOD GROUPS (CARBS, PROTEINS, FRUIT AND VEG, DAIRY, FATTY AND SUGARY FOODS)	Ask yourself the following questions while thinking through how you might use ingredients from each of the main food groups: • *What food group does my key ingredient(s) or dish fall into?* • *Which ingredients from each food group might complement my key ingredient(s)?* • *Could I break with the norm by using an unexpected food group in a common dish?*
TEXTURE	A huge part of the meal experience. When thinking about texture, consider: • *Is my key ingredient(s) or dish chewy, smooth, crunchy, wet, dry, tough, soft or light?* • *Which textures might complement my key ingredient(s)?* • *Which ingredients could offer those textures?* • *What unusual textures could I consider introducing?*
AROMATICS / SEASONING	Spices, herbs and seasonings can round out the flavour of a dish. When thinking about aromatics, consider: • *What is the base flavour of my key ingredient(s)? Is it sweet, warming, salty, bland?* • *Which spices and herbs typically work well with my key ingredient(s)?* • *How could I use herbs and spices to balance the natural flavours of my dish?* • *How could I experiment with unusual flavours and aromas?*
SWEET	Sweetness isn't purely the domain of desserts. When considering if sweetness could play a part in your dish, consider: • *Is your dish already sweet? Or perhaps bitter?* • *Could your dish benefit from added sweetness? Consider how sweetness alters the flavour of nuts, spicy foods or bland salads.* • *Which ingredients could you use to add sweetness – maybe honey, syrup or fruit?*
ACID	When considering the acidity of your dish, think about: • *Is your dish already acidic? Does it contain citrus or vinegar, for example?* • *Does your dish contain fatty elements that could benefit from the cut-through of an acidic ingredient?* • *What acidic ingredients might you introduce – perhaps a citrusy dressing or wine vinegar?*

PHASE 5 RECIPES

In the recipes for this phase, I am going to explore some expert hacks that will make everything on your plate just that bit more exciting, for ever. We're going to master leftover roast meat with an amazing five-spice noodle bowl, break the breakfast rut with a chocolate chip tropical muesli, and crack healthy snacking with a "bit of everything" snack plate.

We will also tackle side dishes head-on with a creamy tzatziki, perfect herby mashed potato, egg-fried quinoa, and quick-pickled cucumbers with fennel and chilli.

Phase 5 meal plans

Opposite are your final two meal plans for use during Phase 5.

Because we're looking at some core staples during this phase – such as dips, breads and vegetable sides – you'll need to think creatively about what you want to enjoy them with and add your own ideas for those to the plan, as well as filling in the blank slots. In this phase, you really are in the driving seat.

WEEK 1

	BREAKFAST	LUNCH	DINNER
MONDAY	CHOCOLATE CHIP TROPICAL MUESLI		
TUESDAY			CRUNCHY FALAFEL PITTAS
WEDNESDAY			CHILLI SESAME BROCCOLI WITH _____
THURSDAY	CLASSIC GREEN SMOOTHIE		
FRIDAY			PERFECT TZATZIKI WITH _____
SATURDAY		SMOKED SAUSAGE AND VEG TRAY BAKE	
SUNDAY		PERFECT HERBY MASHED POTATO WITH _____	

WEEK 2

	BREAKFAST	LUNCH	DINNER
MONDAY			FIVE-SPICE PORK NOODLE BOWL
TUESDAY			QUICK-PICKLED RIBBON CUCUMBERS WITH FENNEL AND CHILLI WITH _____
WEDNESDAY			EGG-FRIED QUINOA WITH _____
THURSDAY			BIT-OF-EVERYTHING SNACK PLATE
FRIDAY	BAKED EGG BREAKFAST ROLLS		
SATURDAY		SUPER SEEDED WHOLEMEAL LOAF WITH _____	
SUNDAY		CHUNKY PARSNIP SOUP	

PREP TIME: 5 MINS

Chocolate chip tropical muesli

This chocolatey, slightly tropical muesli is made with an easy blend of oats, bran, seeds, dried fruit and chocolate chips. It's far lower in sugar than most store-bought cereals, and can be easily varied each time you make it to keep things interesting.

160g (5¾oz) rolled oats
20g (¾oz) oat bran
20g (¾oz) wheat bran
15g (½oz) pine nuts
35g (1¼oz) pumpkin seeds
50g (1¾oz) sunflower seeds
30g (1oz) chopped dried apricots
30g (1oz) chopped dried pineapple
30g (1oz) dried cranberries
50g (1¾oz) milk chocolate chips

Mix all the ingredients together and store in an airtight container. Enjoy with milk, natural yogurt or fresh fruit.

NEVER-THE-SAME-TWICE BREAKFAST CEREALS

The rules of breakfast cereal are pretty simple. You need to have a grain base – oats, wheat bran, puffed rice or puffed quinoa perhaps – and any additions you make should be dry and, of course, taste great together.

From there, you simply pop your mix into a sealed container and store it in a cool dry place, where it will last for weeks and weeks.

So which flavours and combinations work best? I like to start by thinking about my favourite desserts – such as apple pie, carrot cake or lemon blueberry muffins – then figure out how I can replicate those flavours in a healthy breakfast cereal.

You can use the inspiration table from page 181 to help you think further. You might choose to make up a cereal that combines all of the main food groups:

carb-heavy grains, protein-rich nuts, dried fruit and veg, with honey and dairy to serve.

Or you could find inspiration by combining chewy, creamy and crunchy textures, or adding any combination of aromatic, sweet and acidic flavours.

Below are more ideas to inspire your just-add-milk adventures with homemade cereal, so that you never again have to resort to week after week of cornflakes on hurried mornings.

- Dried apples, cinnamon and puffed rice.

- Dried blueberries, chopped hazelnuts and bran flakes.

- Banana chips, peanuts, dried strawberries and mini wheat biscuits.

- Dried cherries, dried apricots, chia seeds and puffed quinoa.

- Dried pineapple, chopped walnuts, coconut flakes and cornflakes.

- Shredded coconut, raisins, cocoa and oats (serve hot).

- Chopped dried dates, puffed rice and popcorn.

- Toasted pumpkin seeds, mixed spice and steel-cut oats (serve hot).

- Chopped macadamia nuts, white chocolate chips and toasted oats.

- Candied lemon peel, dried blueberries and high-fibre bran cereal.

PREP TIME: 5 MINS

Crunchy falafel pittas

Here we're going to take the classic combination of pitta, store-bought falafel and hummus up another couple of notches with creamy avocado, crunchy red pepper, cool mozzarella and a dash of chilli sauce.

4 pitta breads, halved

8 tablespoons hummus (bought or homemade, see page 117)

12 cooked small falafel, hot or cold

2 avocados, pitted, peeled and cut into small chunks

1 red pepper, deseeded and sliced

125g (4½oz) mozzarella cheese, sliced

2 teaspoons chilli sauce, or sweet chilli sauce if you prefer

Warm the pittas, cut them open and spread with the hummus.

Fill with the falafel, followed by the avocado, red pepper and mozzarella.

Drizzle with chilli sauce and serve.

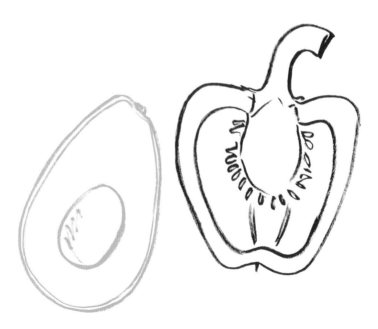

SANDWICHES REIMAGINED

Cheese and tomato, tuna and sweetcorn, BLT...we all have our favourite, don't we?

The humble sandwich is one of the simplest and quickest meals we can make. The downside? Its convenience means we can easily end up in a rut.

Again, use the inspiration table on page 181 to help you start thinking creatively. For example, carbs in the form of bread are the most common feature of a sandwich, but what else would work? How could thinking about the different texture options help you to come up with new filling combinations?

Below are some sandwich combinations to consider. Which of them appeal most? What might you add, change or tweak to make a new, exciting sandwich your family will love?

- Poached egg, Gruyère cheese and sliced gherkins on white bread.

- Spanish omelette, salad and mayo in a wholemeal bap.

- A breakfast-themed tortilla with scrambled egg, walnuts and chives.

- Shredded cabbage, mushroom pâté and coriander in a crusty baguette.

- Carrot slices, pepper, hummus and edamame in a wholemeal bap.

- Cream cheese, sliced apple and cranberry sauce on a toasted bagel.

- Lime-and-chilli-marinated tofu slices, coriander salad and chopped peanuts in a steamed bun.

- Brie, plum chutney and baby spinach in a toasted baguette.

- Smoked salmon, avocado slices and dill cottage cheese in a sliced croissant.

- Prawns, shredded kale and mayo on a thick slice of seeded bread.

PREP TIME: 5 MINS

Chilli-sesame broccoli

Tenderstem broccoli is a wonderful veg with a gentler, sweeter flavour than regular broccoli. If you ever have any left over, this recipe is next-level delicious. With honey to enhance the sweetness, chilli for heat and sesame for earthy crunch, it is far and away one of my favourite ways to jazz up broccoli.

200g (7oz) raw or leftover cooked
    Tenderstem broccoli
1 tablespoon vegetable oil
1 teaspoon sesame seeds
⅛ teaspoon chilli flakes
2 teaspoons honey

If the broccoli is not already cooked, blanch it in a saucepan of boiling water for 2 minutes, then drain.

Warm the oil in a nonstick frying pan over a medium heat. Add the broccoli and fry for 2 minutes, tossing occasionally.

Now add the sesame seeds, chilli flakes and honey. Stir well.

Put the lid on the pan and fry for 1 further minute. Serve!

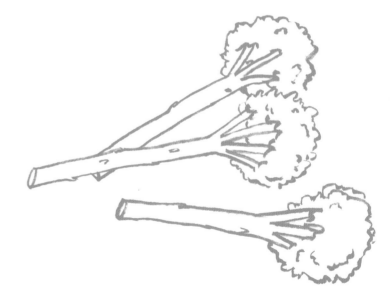

MORE LOW-EFFORT WAYS TO ADD INTEREST TO LEFTOVER VEG

The simple recipe opposite should get you thinking about how else to add interest to humble veg leftovers. Allow your mind to whirr with thoughts of how you might add herbs and spices. How you could chop veg in new ways. How to add protein or fats. How you might bake after boiling, or grill after frying. How you could brighten the flavours with citrus, or soften and enrich the dish with a sauce.

Now refer back to the inspiration table on page 181 to help keep your creativity flowing.

Below are some ideas for pepping up the most common leftover veg. Which might you try in the coming weeks? And what would you add?

- Leftover boiled butternut squash: cubed and fried with sage.

- Unused green leaves such as spinach or kale: wilted with pine nuts and Parmesan cheese.

- Old courgettes: shave into ribbons, spread with feta, roll up and bake.

- Leftover boiled cauliflower: toss in spices and roast.

- Leftover peas: purée with mint leaves.

- Unused root veg: slice very thinly, spray with oil and bake for mixed veg crisps.

- Unused carrots and parsnips: spiralize and toss in crème fraîche and mustard for a simple slaw.

- Leftover baked potatoes: slice, layer up in a roasting tin, cover with a white sauce and grated cheese and bake for a quick gratin.

- Leftover mashed potato: adventurous bubble and squeak, using the potato to hold together any other cooked veg you have in stock – the wilder the better!

- Unused lettuce or cabbage: cut into wedges, drizzle with lime juice and oil, then roast.

Classic green smoothie

An easy way to pack a few of your essential daily vegetables into a single drink. You can't taste the spinach here, but as ever this isn't about hiding veg, it's about celebrating it in all its forms. I recommend getting the kids involved so they can watch the multicoloured jug of fruit and veg being transformed to a pleasing green hue.

1 small or ½ medium pineapple, peeled, cored and roughly chopped
1 mango, peeled, pitted and roughly chopped
2 bananas, peeled
150g (5½oz) baby spinach
200ml (7fl oz) apple juice
handful of ice cubes

Put all the ingredients in a food processor or smoothie maker, blitz, then enjoy.

SMOOTHIES FOR DAYS AND DAYS

Once you experience the Classic Green Smoothie opposite and taste for yourself how effectively vegetables can work in a drink, it's just the beginning.

A smoothie can be almost a complete meal in a glass, incorporating carbohydrate, protein, fruit, veg, dairy and healthy fats. You can make it tart with lemon juice, warm with chilli, savoury with salad, creamy with banana or thick with blueberries.

Explore your own ideas using the inspiration table on page 181. Now it's time to experiment. How would the combinations below turn out if blitzed with ice? What might you change to tweak the colour, thickness, nutritional value or flavour?

- Avocado, cocoa, yogurt, milk and honey.

- Oats, carrot, courgette, mixed spice, apple juice and maple syrup.

- Pistachios, saffron, yogurt, milk and honey.

- Celery, apple, mint and lime juice.

- Seedless watermelon, lime juice and pineapple.

- Tomatoes, celery, chilli and lemon juice.

- Soaked cashews, grape juice and banana.

- Coconut water, mango and mint.

- Raspberries, blueberries, cauliflower and apple juice.

- Cucumber, apple, honeydew melon and water.

Perfect tzatziki

Here is a great example of what happens when you start embracing texture – taste it when you first make it, then let the flavours mature and taste it again...something magical happens to both flavour and texture. This traditional Greek dip goes wonderfully with grilled meats and is perfect at a summer barbecue.

125g (4½oz) natural yogurt

3 tablespoons finely chopped mint leaves

2 garlic cloves, finely chopped

½ tablespoon lemon juice

140g (5oz) cucumber, peeled, deseeded and grated

salt and pepper

Put the yogurt, mint, garlic, lemon juice and cucumber in a bowl. Mix well and allow the flavours to develop for at least 15 minutes.

Season to taste and enjoy.

SIMPLE SAUCES, DIPS AND DRESSINGS TO ROCK YOUR MEALTIMES

That little bowl on the side of your plate is a powerful thing. It will add to and elevate your meals, or balance or round out the flavours, while adding moisture to dishes. Dressings liven up salads and awaken your taste buds; sauces bring the perfect balance of creaminess and zing to cooked meats; and dips take a plate of fries from good to great. In some cases, they can even steal the show: hummus platter, anyone?

So, when you're thinking about creating a dip, dressing or sauce for yourself, there are always two key considerations:

What am I serving it with?
What do I want it to contribute to the meal?

Now cast your mind back to the inspiration table we looked at on page 181. How might you use your sauce to round out the existing food groups in your meal? How could you use dairy and fats to complement the textures? Will you introduce spice or acidity? And how might you balance that with sweetness?

Use these notes as your inspiration to build up your dip, dressing or sauce, tasting as you go. Below are some combinations to explore. Could you develop them into full recipes?

- Dijon mustard, grapefruit juice and agave syrup.

- Mashed avocado with chilli flakes and lime juice.

- Yogurt, mayo and fennel seeds.

- Vinegar, sugar and dill.

- Maple syrup, Dijon mustard and lemon juice.

- Chilli oil, white wine vinegar and honey.

- Blue cheese, crème fraîche, crushed garlic and chives.

- Almond butter, soy sauce, garlic and lime juice.

- Mashed black beans, cream cheese and coriander leaves.

- Pesto, soured cream and cracked black pepper.

PREP TIME: 5 MINS • COOK TIME: 30 MINS

Smoked sausage and veg tray bake

Tray bakes are a dream for those who hate washing up, as everything goes onto a single large baking tray, ready to serve up. This simple meal is served with a dill mayo. It takes just minutes to prepare and the results are incredibly moreish.

For the tray bake
200g (7oz) smoked sausage, sliced into
    2.5cm (1in) pieces
150g (5½oz) sweet potato, peeled and finely
    chopped
150g (5½oz) butternut squash, peeled,
    deseeded and chopped into chunks
1 onion, finely chopped
½ red cabbage, cut into thin wedges
1 head of broccoli, cut into 2.5cm (1in) florets
3 tablespoons finely chopped sage leaves
2 tablespoons olive oil
salt and pepper

For the creamy dill dip
6 tablespoons mayonnaise
3 tablespoons finely chopped dill
a little whole milk (optional)

Preheat the oven to 200°C (400°F), 180°C fan, Gas Mark 6.

Put the sausage, chopped vegetables and sage into a large baking tray.

Drizzle the oil on top, season well, then mix with your hands and spread out in a single layer.

Bake for 20 minutes, then give the tray a little shake and bake for a further 10 minutes until everything is cooked and sizzling.

Mix the mayonnaise and dill together, season to taste, then serve in a bowl alongside the sausages and veg. If you'd like your dip to be more of a dressing, just stir in a splash of milk until loosened.

ONE BAKING TRAY, ENDLESS IDEAS

Once I learned how easy it was to create an entire meal on a single baking tray, I was immediately keen to explore many more combinations.

Let's look to our inspiration table once again (see page 181). The key consideration is that everything needs to cook at same time, so be careful to choose the right combination so that nothing is over- or undercooked.

Baking trays are great for building up a balance of food groups, so think about how you'll use carbs and protein, fruit and veg, and how you might introduce dairy, such as in the dressing we made for the smoked sausage.

You can play with texture by thinking about cooking time as well as ingredients. How might you add moisture, crunch or chew? And how might spices or a dash of citrus lift the whole meal?

Below are some combinations to experiment with.

- Extra-firm tofu, carrot, onion, bok choy, ginger, cashews, courgette noodles, lime and sesame seeds.

- Sweet potato, lean minced beef, garlic, green peppers, onions and chilli.

- Pork chops, sweet potato, broccoli and honeyed rhubarb.

- Chicken breast, artichoke hearts, parsnip, rosemary and bay leaf.

- Gnocchi, red peppers, baby plum tomatoes, green beans and pesto.

- Grated potato, mushrooms, tomatoes, bacon, sausage and eggs.

- Sweetcorn, new potatoes, prawns and stock.

- "Rainbow baking sheet": cherry tomatoes, carrots, yellow peppers, broccoli, purple potatoes and radicchio.

- Meatballs, spinach, sprouts, tomatoes and chopped potatoes.

- Strawberries, bread cubes, cinnamon, crème fraîche and honey.

PREP TIME: 5 MINS • COOK TIME: 20 MINS

Perfect herby mashed potato

Whether you top it with a knob of butter or smother it with gravy, great mash is essential. There are a few tricks to preparing mash so that it's never gluey, lumpy or gritty. Nail these, and you've opened the door to a world of amazing mashes!

1kg (2lb 4oz) floury potatoes (such as
   Maris Piper), peeled and cut into
   even-sized chunks
50ml (1¾fl oz) whole milk
2 tablespoons slightly salted butter
2½ tablespoons finely chopped parsley leaves
salt and pepper

Rinse the potatoes well to remove the surface starch and prevent your mash becoming gluey. Put them in a saucepan and cover with cold water.

Place over a high heat and bring to the boil, then reduce the heat to a simmer and cook for 15–20 minutes. Don't boil too rapidly – this could mean your potatoes cook too fast on the outside before they're cooked in the middle.

To check your potatoes are cooked through, stab one with the point of a knife. If it slides in easily, the potatoes are ready.

Drain the potatoes well, then return to the pan and mash thoroughly. Add the milk, butter and herbs and mash a little further to combine. Season to taste and serve.

MASH THAT'S NEVER BORING

A reliable way to make a common staple turn out great every time is, of course, a wonderful thing, but by now we know that's no excuse to get too comfortable. I'm not suggesting we turn our backs on good old mashed potato, but by exploring a wide variety of additions, we can play with texture, flavour, seasonings and more to discover almost endless combinations.

Get inspired by thinking about how each major food group might be incorporated into your mash; consider how to introduce crunchy or chewy textures with nuts and veg, and which additions would bring sweetness, spice or acidity.

On the right are 10 ideas to get you thinking about more ways to mash up your next meal.

- Skin-on mash: leave the potato skins on for lots of extra flavour and a great texture.

- Sweet potato mash: replace the white potato with sweet potato and reduce the cooking time to 10–15 minutes.

- Cheesy mash: add cream cheese or grated cheese for an indulgent mash.

- Half and half: root veg such as parsnip, swede and celeriac, as well as squashes such as butternut, offer fantastic flavours, but their textures don't always lend themselves well to mashing. Try replacing half the potato with another veg for a great mixed veg mash.

- Mash 'n' stuff: mash loves additions, so try throwing in wilted greens, fried mushrooms, pine nuts or chopped walnuts for a whole new experience.

- No-waste mash: why throw away the skins? Wash your spuds well before peeling and, while they're bubbling away, pop the peels onto an oiled roasting tray, season well and roast. Serve these crispy, delicious treats on top of your mash.

- Multi-spiced mash: divide your mash between two (or more) saucepans and add a different spice to each. Ground turmeric or cumin are a good place to start as they inject both flavour and colour, which means more fun at dinner time.

- Mediterranean mash: stir in sliced sun-dried tomatoes, roasted peppers or olives for a mash with a taste of the Med. Finish with a little pesto on top.

- Quick mash cakes: combine any type of mash with other chopped leftover veg, form into patties and fry lightly in a little olive oil, turning once, for easy, quick potato cakes.

- Mash pancakes: combine mashed potato with pancake batter and fry by the ladleful for a tasty potato accompaniment to your next cooked breakfast.

Five-spice pork noodle bowl

Slippery noodles, crunchy veg and aromatic pork – this is the perfect Monday night dinner, using up leftover pork from a Sunday roast. Five spice is a wonderful Chinese blend of star anise, cloves, Chinese cinnamon, Sichuan pepper and fennel seeds. It pairs beautifully with fatty pork. You'll need a few pans on the go, but this is really quick and the results are fabulous.

2 large free-range eggs

800ml (28fl oz) water

1 chicken stock cube (ideally reduced salt)

½ teaspoon five spice powder

3cm (1¼in) fresh root ginger, thinly sliced

2 garlic cloves, thinly sliced

1 tablespoon soy sauce (reduced-salt, if available)

2 heads of bok choy, cut in half lengthways

½ tablespoon vegetable oil

250g (9oz) cooked pork, cubed

250g (9oz) soba noodles

1 carrot, cut into matchsticks

8 radishes, thinly sliced

1 tablespoon sesame seeds

3 spring onions, thinly sliced

1 red chilli, thinly sliced (optional)

Place the eggs in a medium saucepan, cover with cold water, bring to the boil, then turn off the heat, replace the lid and leave for 6 minutes. Lift out of the water, allow to cool, then peel and cut in half.

Meanwhile, bring the measured water to the boil in a large saucepan. Add the stock cube, five spice, ginger, garlic and soy sauce, then reduce the heat and simmer for 5 minutes. Add the bok choy and simmer for a further 5 minutes.

Warm the oil in a nonstick frying pan over a medium heat, then add the pork and fry for 3–5 minutes until browned and heated through.

Cook the noodles according to the packet instructions, then drain and divide between 4 bowls. Lift the bok choy from the stock and divide between the bowls.

Top each of the bowls with the carrot, radishes, pork and half an egg, then ladle the piping hot stock over the top.

Finish with a sprinkling of sesame seeds and a scattering of spring onions. Add the chilli if you'd like a spicier meal.

GETTING CREATIVE WITH COOKED MEATS

I'm sure you're no stranger to the joys of leftover cooked meat, but as this gorgeous noodle bowl shows, there are lots more ways to reinvigorate it than to pop it between two slices of bread.

Let's have a look at the inspiration table again (see page 181). Consider how you might use a wet texture to balance the risk of dryness in cooked meat. How might an aromatic marinade reintroduce flavour? How could you use citrus to cut through any fattiness? How could meat be used to add protein to a vegetable-based dish, rather than to be the star of the show?

Here are 10 ways you could create new dishes.

- Cut meat into strips and stir-fry with sliced onion, sweet peppers and smoked paprika. Serve with tortillas for an impromptu taco night.

- Make a basic pasta sauce by frying the meat in chunks with onion and garlic, then adding tomatoes and simmering.

- Jazz up instant noodles at lunch by stirring in a little leftover meat and topping with fresh veg.

- Pop the meat, your choice of veg and either gravy or white sauce into a pie tin, top with ready-rolled puff pastry and bake for a super-quick pot pie.

- Fry leftover minced or shredded beef with onions, garlic and barbecue sauce, toss in chopped tomatoes and serve in rolls for quick sloppy joes.

- Add chunks of leftover meat to canned, frozen or leftover soup before gently heating for a more filling, protein-rich meal.

- Heat leftover beef with mushrooms, cream and parsley.

- Place leftover cooked and sliced meat on a baking tray and pop into a super-low oven preheated to 60°C (140°F), 40° fan, Gas Mark ¼, or as low as it will go. Cook for several hours and you'll have jerky.

- Pop tougher cuts of leftover meat into a slow cooker with veg and stock and cook on low for eight hours to tenderize.

- Cut cold cuts into small chunks and stir into chopped salads.

PREP TIME: 5 MINS • COOK TIME: 5 MINS

Quick-pickled ribbon cucumbers with fennel and chilli

Proper pickles are fermented over time for a deep flavour, but quick pickling gives a gentler piquancy in a fraction of the time. You can add sugar for vegetables that benefit from extra sweetness, while introducing spices and herbs can create all sorts of exciting new flavours.

280g (10oz) cucumber, cut into ribbons with a vegetable peeler (discard the very seedy middle)
100ml (3½fl oz) white wine vinegar
½ teaspoon salt
1½ teaspoons caster sugar
¼ teaspoon fennel seeds
¼ teaspoon chilli flakes
100ml (3½fl oz) water

Clean a 300ml (10fl oz) lidded, heatproof jar – ideally one straight from the hot cycle of the dishwasher so that it is sterilized.

Pack the cucumber into the jar, making sure it is at least 2cm (¾in) shy of the top.

In a small pan, mix the vinegar with the salt, sugar, fennel seeds, chilli flakes and the measured water. Place over a medium heat and bring to the boil, then pour into the jar, almost up to the top.

Double-check that the vegetables are totally submerged.

Leave to cool on the counter, then tighten the lid and place in the fridge for 48 hours before cracking open to enjoy. Kept in the refrigerator, they will last for a couple of weeks.

THE SECRET WORLD OF QUICK PICKLING

Cucumbers are a great introduction to quick pickling, but the vegetables you use and how you cut them is up to you. Of course, the thicker you cut them, the less the vinegar will be able to penetrate the flesh in 48 hours, so choose wisely.

Salads and non-starchy veg can be pickled raw. Green vegetables benefit from a brief blanching: boil them for 2–3 minutes, then plunge into cold water to help them retain their vibrant colour.

Use the inspiration table on page 181 to think about the flavours you might use. Pickles are, of course, primarily about acid and crunch, so you can also have fun thinking about food groups, texture and flavour when you come to decide what you're going to pair them with.

Here are some ideas for your next quick pickling experiments.

- Beetroot and onion.

- Carrots and coriander seeds.

- Pears, apples and cloves.

- Cauliflower and capers.

- Garlic cloves and sliced chillies.

- Watermelon and mint.

- Radishes and carrots.

- Endives and shallots.

- Carrots and ginger.

- Cannellini beans with black pepper.

PREP TIME: 5 MINS • COOK TIME: 30 MINS

Egg-fried quinoa

It's time to try quinoa... When you step outside your regular choice of grain – rice, in this case – you open up a whole new set of meals. This egg-fried quinoa is higher in protein than rice and works wonderfully as an accompaniment to all sorts of meals, or even as a quick lunch on its own.

160g (5¾oz) quinoa, rinsed and drained

2 tablespoons olive oil

2cm (¾in) fresh root ginger, cut into slivers

100g (3½oz) mangetout

100g (3½oz) baby sweetcorn, cut into 2cm (¾in) pieces

50g (1¾oz) cashews

1 teaspoon five spice powder

4 large free-range eggs, lightly beaten

salt and pepper

Cook the quinoa according to the packet instructions.

Meanwhile, warm the oil in a nonstick frying pan over a medium-high heat. Add the ginger, mangetout and baby sweetcorn and fry for 5 minutes until the corn begins to take on some colour and the mange-tout begins to puff up slightly.

Add the cooked quinoa, cashews and five spice and stir through.

Make a well in the middle of your quinoa mixture and pour the eggs in, stirring gently within the well for 1 minute. Once a few curds form, fold everything together and continue to cook for 2–4 minutes. At first, the quinoa will seem sloppy, but it will firm up as the eggs cook through – try not to overcook them.

Season to taste and serve.

A TOOLKIT TO JAZZ UP YOUR GRAINS

The beauty of grains and pseudograins (such as quinoa, which is in fact a seed) is that they can bulk out a meal and make it filling and satisfying.

Use the inspiration table on page 181 to think about the main grains available to you, and how you might combine them with other ingredients.

Start with the major food groups and consider how you might introduce meats, tofu, fruit, veg and dairy. Will grains be an addition or the star of the show? How might you add spice, sweetness or zing?

On the right are 10 ideas to help you turn every portion of grains into something extra special.

- Quinoa, chopped tomatoes, coriander and sliced jalapeños.

- Sweetcorn, feta, pistachios, figs and honey.

- Bulgur wheat, parsley, lemon juice and pomegranate seeds.

- Buckwheat, spring onions, chilli, lime juice, mint and crushed peanuts.

- Egg-fried wild rice with peas and sriracha.

- Buckwheat, lardons, chopped apple and sage.

- Sweetcorn, roast squash and sage.

- Quinoa, avocado, coriander and cashews.

- Pearl barley, chorizo, chopped egg and coriander.

- Couscous, chopped pineapple, chopped ham and five spice.

PREP TIME: 5 MINS

Bit-of-everything snack plate

Perfect for bridging the hungry gap between getting home from school and the evening meal, this balanced selection of ingredients is just enough to share between four without ruining dinner. We have rice cakes for carbs; hummus and eggs for protein; sliced peppers for veg; mozzarella for dairy; avocado for fat; and nuts and seeds for a vitamin boost and crunch. Let's dig in.

4 rice cakes

4 tablespoons hummus (bought or homemade, see page 117)

1 red pepper, deseeded and sliced

125g (4½oz) mozzarella cheese, sliced

½ avocado, peeled, pitted and sliced

1 tablespoon mixed nuts and seeds

1 medium free-range egg, soft-boiled (see page 137)

Place all the ingredients on a large plate so that everyone can help themselves. Take an extra moment to arrange everything attractively – remember, the first bite is taken with the eye, and a little beauty makes this simple snack so much more appealing.

CRACKING HEALTHY SNACKING

Snacking is often seen as unhealthy, but once you know how, I think it's just about the easiest way to eat healthily. Why? Because you can literally build the healthy plate diagram (see page 25) with real foods on your plate, whizzing around your refrigerator and cupboards to grab elements that tick all the boxes for a nutritious meal.

And since it's a snack, you don't even have to worry about whether each element mixes with the others. There'll be no cooking: you just have to like the look of it all, check it'll satisfy all your flavour and texture cravings, then serve it up and let everyone dig in.

Refer to the inspiration table on page 181 to think about how you might introduce crunchy, wet, smooth, chewy and firm textures onto a single snack plate.

Think about strongly flavoured elements balanced with light or citrusy ones.

Remember to keep varying your plates from snack to snack and including a more challenging food each time in order to sustain your commitment to variation. Below are some ideas to illustrate how you might create some really delicious, varied plates from things you find in the refrigerator and cupboards.

- French bread, pesto, tomatoes, leftover greens and roast chicken.

- Pumpernickel bread, gravlax, pickled cabbage, cream cheese and chives.

- Flatbread, leftover roast lamb, mixed peppers, tomato, yogurt and mint.

- Rye crackers, figs, hazelnuts, sliced apples, cheese and grapes.

- Mini rice cakes, pears, baby spinach, nut butter and mixed seeds.

- Soda bread, sliced sausage, onions, gherkins and sauerkraut.

- Cold brown rice, soy sauce, avocado, smoked mackerel, cucumber and pumpkin seeds.

- Mini baked potatoes, edamame, marinated tofu, feta and pickled beetroot.

- Toast, poached eggs, ham, cannellini beans and sun-dried tomatoes.

- Tortilla triangles, leftover cooked onions and peppers, grated cheese, cooked chicken, salad leaves and smoked paprika.

PREP TIME: 10 MINS • COOK TIME: 15 MINS

Baked egg breakfast rolls

This really special breakfast makes use of leftovers again, by stuffing a lovely crusty roll with cooked sausages and bacon, spinach, tomatoes and pine nuts before cracking in an egg and baking. When you cut into the crisp crust on these beauties, the yolk will ooze luxuriously into the meat and vegetables.

4 crusty bread rolls

1 tablespoon olive oil

4 cooked sausages, cut into 1.5cm (⅝in) slices

2 cooked bacon rashers, finely chopped

160g (5¾oz) baby spinach

2 medium tomatoes, chopped

40g (1½oz) pine nuts

4 large free-range eggs

salt and pepper

Preheat the oven to 200°C (400°F), 180°C fan, Gas Mark 6.

Cut off the top off each of the rolls and scoop out most of the bready centre (you can blitz this in a food processor and freeze the breadcrumbs for another recipe). Place the shells on a baking tray.

Warm the oil in a nonstick frying pan over a medium heat. Add the sausages and bacon and fry for 2–3 minutes, just to reheat.

Add the spinach, tomatoes and pine nuts and fry for a further 2 minutes or until everything is fully heated through.

Season with salt and pepper and spoon evenly into the rolls, leaving any excess liquid in the pan.

Crack an egg into each roll and place in the oven for 15 minutes, until cooked. Sprinkle with pepper and serve.

A DOZEN EGGS, ENDLESS WAYS

Eggs are one of my favourite ingredients in creative cooking because they're just so versatile – few ingredients can be used in so many ways. You can enjoy them scrambled, fried, coddled, poached, devilled and boiled, of course, but also in omelettes and soufflés, in quiches, stirred into rice and in a thousand other ways. And any one of these options can itself be customized endlessly.

It can help to think about the different textures that egg can lend to a dish. For example, a runny, soft-boiled egg yolk can act as a natural sauce for firm vegetables, or you can balance dense proteins with a fluffy, light scramble. And could thinking about flavour push you outside your comfort zone? How about a sweet omelette?

Let's get inspired to use eggs in more ways than just sunny side up using the inspiration table on page 181. Below are some ideas to inspire your eggs-periments.

- Three-mushroom scramble: oyster, shiitake and chestnut.

- Smoked salmon and asparagus scramble

- Scrambled egg and mashed avocado on toast.

- Ultimate breakfast frittata: egg, bacon, sausage, tomato and black pudding.

- Individual frittatas: like the one on page 45 but made in a muffin tray.

- Halloumi-chorizo frittata with basil.

- Mini quiches in a muffin tin: ready-rolled shortcrust pastry, eggs, milk, spinach, chopped ham and tomatoes.

- Quiche in a pepper: hollow out a pepper and fill with a quiche filling mixture before baking.

- Carrot and coriander omelette.

- Boiled egg with multicoloured soldiers: avocado-topped toast, tapenade-topped toast, tomato-spread topped toast.

Super seeded wholemeal loaf

From pizza to soda bread, challah to focaccia, tortillas and more, in your journey so far you've already made some wonderful breads. To round things off, you're going to make my tried and true wholemeal seeded loaf with pine nuts. It's simple, but comes out of the tin looking like it's fresh from a bakery.

4 teaspoons pumpkin seeds

4 teaspoons sunflower seeds

4 teaspoons pine nuts

500g (1lb 2oz) strong wholemeal bread flour, plus extra for dusting

7g (¼oz) fast-action dried yeast

1 teaspoon salt

300ml (10fl oz) lukewarm water

Mix the seeds and nuts together in a small bowl. In a large bowl, mix the flour, yeast, all but 1 tablespoon of the seed and nut mix and the salt.

Make a well in the middle and pour in the lukewarm water. Mix with a fork to roughly combine.

Turn onto a floured work surface and knead for 5 minutes. The dough will be very sticky at first but will soon start to come away from your hands, remaining only a little tacky.

Tuck the dough into itself underneath, then shape it into a rectangle the same length as a nonstick 500g (1lb) loaf tin. Wet the top of the dough with a little water, then sprinkle the remaining nuts and seeds on the work surface and roll the dough over them so that they stick to the top.

Turn right side up and place in your loaf tin. Put the whole thing in a large ziplock bag with plenty of room to double in size and place somewhere warm for 1 hour to prove.

When the dough is almost proved, preheat the oven to 200°C (400°F), 180°C fan, Gas Mark 6. Remove the loaf from the ziplock bag and place in the centre of the oven for 25 minutes, or until golden brown.

Tip the loaf out of the tin and gently tap the base – if it sounds hollow, it's cooked through. Leave to cool on a wire rack. If you wish, you can put a towel around your bread while cooling to produce a softer crust.

GEARING UP TO BE BOLD WITH BREAD

Breadmaking is a rewarding craft with endless possibilities – you can make bread anything from sweet to savoury, chewy to floaty-light. So settle down with a slice of toast and use the inspiration table on page 181 to help you come up with new ideas.

Think about alternative grains, such as oats, millet or puffed quinoa. Consider how you might add chewy dried fruit, crunchy seeds or creamy chocolate chips to a loaf to alter its texture. Or how you might play with flavour to create loaves bursting with aromatic herbs and spices. On the right are 10 ideas to get you started.

- Candied peel, dried fruits and mixed spice wholemeal loaf.

- Basil, oregano and sun-dried tomato rolls.

- Mixed herb and Parmesan cheese challah (see page 99).

- Goats' cheese and nettle pesto focaccia (see page 83).

- Cranberry and sage dinner rolls.

- Onion and olive soda bread.

- Basil-flecked pizza dough (see page 37).

- Walnut, raisin and chocolate chip loaf.

- Mexican spiced tortillas.

- Ginger and lemon granary loaf.

PREP TIME: 5 MINS • COOK TIME: 25 MINS

Chunky parsnip soup

In a single bowl, soup can deliver all sorts of textures, flavours, colours and aromas, making for a truly satisfying and effortlessly healthy meal. This recipe is fantastic: herby and chunky.

2 tablespoons olive oil

1 onion, finely chopped

1 celery stick, finely chopped

1 carrot, finely chopped

1 rosemary sprig

3 tablespoons sage leaves

250g (9oz) potatoes, peeled and chopped
into 2.5cm (1in) pieces

450g (1lb) parsnips, scrubbed and chopped
into 2.5cm (1in) pieces

750ml (26fl oz) vegetable stock (ideally
reduced-salt)

small handful of coriander leaves,
finely chopped

salt and pepper

Pour the oil into a large nonstick saucepan over a medium heat. Add the onion, celery, carrot and a pinch of salt and pepper and fry gently for 5 minutes until softened. Add the rosemary and sage and fry for a further minute.

Add the potatoes, parsnips and stock, bring to the boil, then reduce the heat to a simmer for 20 minutes.

Remove the rosemary sprig, ladle the soup into a food processor and pulse until just broken down – don't overblend, or the texture might become gluey. If it looks too thick, add some water to loosen.

Return to the pan, add the coriander leaves, heat through and serve.

HOW TO MAKE ANY SOUP DELICIOUS

How we choose to cook a soup is almost as important as the ingredients themselves. Think of it like this: boiled potatoes and fries are made from the same ingredient, but taste quite different. Raw garlic is quite different from the roasted version. Boiled cabbage is mellow, while roasted cabbage can be sweetly bitter.

When creating a soup, then, think not only about the ingredients you wish to use, but in what form you want to use them to maximize the flavours with a complementary set of textures, aromas and tastes.

Finally, decide if you want to blitz your soup smooth or leave it chunky; both can be great – it's about what you think you'll love most.

Use the inspiration table on page 181 to store your notes as you start experimenting. Go by taste, texture and eye. If you wish, you can add a squeeze of citrus or pinch of seasoning to a spoonful of the soup before committing to adding it to the whole pan. Then, just keep adding gradually and testing until you're happy with the result.

Hungry for more? Here are 10 more combinations to try.

- Roasted beetroot chunks, vegetable stock and crème fraîche.

- Roasted pumpkin chunks, vegetable stock and peanut butter.

- Dried red lentils, vegetable stock and a little Parmesan cheese.

- Curry spices, cauliflower, vegetable stock and soaked cashews.

- Potatoes, garlic, peas, mint, lemon juice and stock.

- Broccoli, stock, milk, paprika, mustard and cheese.

- Roasted tomatoes, milk, garlic, basil and cayenne.

- Sweet potato, stock, chilli and coconut milk.

- Tomato passata, kidney beans, butter beans, haricot beans, black beans, cannellini beans, garlic, paprika, cumin and stock (leave this chunky).

- Chestnut mushrooms, garlic, fresh thyme, stock and cream.

PHASE 5 REFLECTION JOURNAL

RECIPE	DATE TRIED	SOMETHING YOU LIKED	SOMETHING YOU LIKED LESS	WHAT TO CHANGE NEXT TIME
CHOCOLATE CHIP TROPICAL MUESLI				
CRUNCHY FALAFEL PITTAS				
CHILLI SESAME BROCCOLI				
CLASSIC GREEN SMOOTHIE				
PERFECT TZATZIKI				
SMOKED SAUSAGE AND VEG TRAY BAKE				
PERFECT HERBY MASHED POTATO				

RECIPE	DATE TRIED	SOMETHING YOU LIKED	SOMETHING YOU LIKED LESS	WHAT TO CHANGE NEXT TIME
FIVE-SPICE PORK NOODLE BOWL				
QUICK-PICKLED RIBBON CUCUMBERS WITH FENNEL AND CHILLI				
EGG-FRIED QUINOA				
BIT-OF-EVERYTHING SNACK PLATE				
BAKED EGG BREAKFAST ROLLS				
SUPER SEEDED WHOLEMEAL LOAF				
CHUNKY PARSNIP SOUP				

CONCLUSION

Your journey is complete! Or just beginning...

When you started reading this book, chances are you were nervous. You'd had a cursory flick through the recipes and thought, "Will my children really ever eat so many different things?" Oh, how far you've come!

When you embarked on Phase 1, you began by gently introducing small elements of unfamiliar colour, flavour or texture into familiar family favourites. You served up curried fish and chips and bean-packed burgers, and you probably saw some resistance but also some successes. And you took your first steps towards helping the whole family to think differently about food.

During Phase 2, you got the kids involved and began to stoke their passion for food. You enjoyed experiments with texture, taste and smell, and you went out and shopped and foraged to help your family gain a better understanding of where their food comes from. Next you celebrated your gathered ingredients with recipes that pushed everyone's foodie expectations a little further.

In Phase 3, you maintained your children's new-found enthusiasm for food by focusing on fun. You experimented with colour, shape and texture and learned how to celebrate mealtimes as occasions. You built enthusiasm for unfamiliar food with arty, colourful, fun dishes, and you used unusual ingredients with confidence.

As you moved into Phase 4, you took on the biggest challenge of all: to serve up 14 dishes that were intentionally surprising, even to adult palates. You braved activities that pushed your family's appetite for variety even further. These activities not only saw you eating food combinations you would never have dreamed of, but also developing your own ideas for wacky yet delicious meals.

In Phase 5, you focused on cementing variety and building on everything you had previously absorbed. You were cooking in a new way, learning to diversify and vary a host of core meals and dishes. With so much already achieved, you learned techniques to keep your family mealtimes varied in the long term. You became your own recipe creator.

Remember, every bit of your journey has been preserved in the scribbles and notes across the pages. This book is now your reference guide, your inspiration and your proud record of achievement. It's here to support you when you need a boost, and to inspire you when you look to create something entirely new.

As challenges present themselves – and they will! – use everything that you've learned and have faith in variety. Stick with it, keep going and it will continue to pay off.

And remember too that I am here to help. I'm still feeding two kids who, just like everyone else, have their fussy moments. I'm still facing the same trials all busy families face. And I'm always happy to share my experiences along the way. Reach out to me on via social profiles or email. Ask questions, suggest ideas, share your journey, send your pics. I would love to hear from you.

Congratulations on your achievement, and here's to many more years of getting your kids to eat anything!

amummytoo.co.uk
fb.com/amummytoo
instagram.com/amummytoo

twitter.com/amummytoo
youtube.com/amummytoocouk
pinterest.com/amummytoo

WEEKLY SHOPPING LISTS

These lists contain everything you need to make the recipes in each phase*. You should accumulate groceries as you progress, so check your cupboards before shopping. If you are feeding more or fewer mouths than each recipe serves, adjust the quantites accordingly.

*I assume you already have salt and pepper.

PHASE 1

WEEK 1

FRUIT & VEGETABLES
8 dessert apples
85g (3oz) Tenderstem broccoli
30g (1oz) red cabbage
450g (1lb) carrots
1 stick celery
9 cloves, or 1 bulb, garlic
2.5cm (1in) fresh root ginger
1 lemon
½ red onion
2 white onions
100g (3½oz) fresh or frozen peas
½ orange pepper
1 red pepper
750g (1lb 10oz) potatoes
100g (3½oz) salad leaves
200g (7oz) spinach
2 spring onions
50g (1¾oz) sugar snap peas
500g (1lb 2oz) sweet potatoes
50g (1¾oz) baby sweetcorn

CUPBOARD
400g (14oz) can kidney beans
400g (14oz) can mixed beans
4–6 wholemeal burger buns
100g (3½oz) dried breadcrumbs
300g (10½oz) strong white bread flour
3 tablespoons honey
250g (9oz) lentils
250g (9oz) black rice or other noodles
350g (12oz) wholewheat pasta
1 tablespoon sesame seeds
1 reduced-salt vegetable stock cube
35g (1¼oz), or 1 small can, sweetcorn
4 x 400g (14oz) cans chopped tomatoes

280g (10oz) jar sun-dried tomatoes in oil
fast-action dried yeast
cornflour
plain flour
gravy granules
olive oil
olive oil spray
vegetable oil
reduced-salt soy sauce

REFRIGERATOR
275g (9¾oz) mozzarella cheese
170g (6oz) Parmesan cheese
200g (7oz) cooked chicken
240g (8½oz) skinless cod fillets
2 eggs
6 tablespoons, or 1 small tub, hummus
200ml (7fl oz) whole milk
400g (14oz) natural yogurt

HERBS & SPICES
basil
chilli powder
chives
ground cinnamon
ground coriander
ground cumin
curry powder
garlic granules
paprika
dried sage
ground turmeric
vanilla extract

WEEK 2

FRUIT & VEGETABLES
1 small head broccoli
2 carrots
1 stick celery
½ red chilli
200g (7oz) fresh or frozen edamame beans
5 cloves, or ½ bulb, garlic
250g (9oz) leeks
1 lemon
1 small lettuce
250g (9oz) Portobello mushrooms
1½ red onions
2½ white onions
100g (3½oz) fresh or frozen peas
6–8 green peppers
½ red pepper
4 baking potatoes
200g (7oz) new potatoes
100g (3½oz) baby spinach
1 beef tomato
100g (3½oz) cherry tomatoes

CUPBOARD
45g (1½oz) blanched almonds
2 x 400g (14oz) cans haricot beans
2 x 400g (14oz) cans kidney beans
4–6 brioche burger buns
130g (4½oz) fresh breadcrumbs
45g (1½oz) cashew nuts
1 small jar gherkins
250g (9oz) red lentils
2½ teaspoons English mustard
350g (12oz) rigatoni pasta
400g (14oz) wholewheat spaghetti
1 reduced-salt beef stock cube
1 reduced-salt vegetable stock cube
5 tablespoons, or 1 tube, tomato purée

5 x 400g (14oz) cans chopped tomatoes
50ml (1¾fl oz) white wine vinegar
plain flour
tomato ketchup
mayonnaise
olive oil
olive oil spray
vegetable oil
brown sugar

REFRIGERATOR
500g (1lb 2oz) minced beef or veggie
   mince
250g (9oz) minced beef
100g (3½oz) Caerphilly cheese
310g (11oz) mature Cheddar cheese
50g (1¾oz) Parmesan cheese
small pot crème fraîche
13 eggs
250ml (9fl oz) whole milk
slightly salted butter

HERBS & SPICES
chilli powder
chives
fresh coriander
ground cumin
mixed herbs
mint
paprika
parsley
dried sage
thyme

PHASE 2
WEEK 1

FRUIT & VEGETABLES
1 avocado
2 bananas
200g (7oz) fresh or frozen mixed berries
150g (5½oz) fresh mixed berries
1 carrot
½ cucumber
1 garlic clove
1 lime
1 red onion

20g (¾oz) rocket
2 large tomatoes
250g (9oz) frozen mixed vegetables

CUPBOARD
2 tablespoons flaked almonds
4 slices wholemeal bread
150g (5½oz) mixed dried fruits
670g (1lb 8oz) self-raising flour
500g (1lb 2oz) strong white bread flour
4½ tablespoons honey
120ml (4fl oz) maple syrup
100g (3½oz) rice vermicelli noodles
150g (5½oz) mixed nuts and seeds
400g (14oz) rolled oats
50g (1¾oz) black olives
50g (1¾oz) green olives
30g (1oz) peanuts
30g (1oz) pine nuts
1 small jar roasted red peppers
12 spring roll wrappers (rice pancakes)
150g (5½oz) jar sun-dried tomatoes in oil
baking powder
bicarbonate of soda
plain flour
mayonnaise
olive oil
olive oil spray
sriracha hot chilli sauce
vegetable oil
fast-action dried yeast

REFRIGERATOR
120g (4½oz) Cheddar cheese
180g (6oz) Gouda cheese
125g (4½oz) mozzarella cheese
65g (2½oz) Parmesan cheese
7 eggs
800g (1lb 12oz) gnocchi
350ml (12fl oz) whole milk
100g (3½oz) cooked prawns
100g (3½oz) firm or extra-firm tofu
650g (1lb 7oz) natural yogurt
butter, slightly salted

HERBS & SPICES
basil
ground cinnamon
ground cumin
garlic granules

wild garlic or chives
mint
ground mixed spice
parsley
dried sage
thyme
vanilla extract

WEEK 2

FRUIT & VEGETABLES
2 dessert apples
1 bunch asparagus
2 bananas
2 boiled beetroot
2 small heads broccoli
10g (¼oz) purple-sprouting broccoli
4 carrots
125g (4½oz) cauliflower
2 sticks celery
1 red chilli
2 courgettes
2 figs
7 cloves, or ½ bulb, garlic
1 kiwifruit
1 lemon
1 lime
1 thick slice honeydew melon
1 red onion
1 white onion
100g (3½oz) pomegranate seeds
1 handful radishes
1 handful raspberries
4 shallots
40g (1½oz) spinach
2 strawberries
10g (¼oz) sugar snap peas
100g (3½oz) baby sweetcorn

CUPBOARD
75g (2¾oz) dried apricots
½ loaf sourdough bread
70g (2½oz) panko breadcrumbs
2 x 400g (14oz) cans chickpeas
100g (3½oz) dark chocolate chips
1 small jar gherkins
1 jar honey
100g (3½oz) mixed nuts and seeds, plus
   2 tablespoons (optional)

2 tablespoons raisins (optional)
250g (9oz) Arborio rice
125g (4½oz) brown rice
1 reduced-salt chicken stock cube
1 reduced-salt vegetable stock cube
400g (14oz) can chopped tomatoes
baking powder
plain flour
olive oil
olive oil spray
vegetable oil
peanut butter
caster sugar
tomato purée
white wine vinegar
fast-action dried yeast

REFRIGERATOR
100g (3½oz) Cheddar cheese
100g (3½oz) Parmesan cheese
40g (1½oz) smoked cheese
640g (1lb 7oz) chicken breast
150ml (5fl oz) soured cream
100g (3½oz) crème fraîche
5 eggs
1 small tub hummus
568ml (1 pint) bottle whole milk
150g (5½oz) natural yogurt
slightly salted butter

HERBS & SPICES
cayenne pepper
chives
fresh coriander
ground cinnamon
ground coriander
ground cumin
ground ginger
English mustard powder
whole (ideally) or ground nutmeg
paprika
ground turmeric

PHASE 3

WEEK 1

FRUIT & VEGETABLES
2 green apples
2 small beetroot
40g (1½oz) red cabbage
3 carrots
750g (1lb 10oz) cauliflower florets
1 stick celery
1½ courgettes
30g (1oz) cucumber
1 bulb garlic
20 red grapes (1 small punnet)
½ lemon
2 Romaine lettuce hearts
1½ limes
2–3 mandarins
2 red onions
1 white onion
200g (7oz) frozen peas
2½ red peppers
1 small tub pomegranate seeds
1 small bag salad leaves
100g (3½oz) spinach
100g (3½oz) sugar snap peas
50g (1¾oz) sweet potato
8 cherry tomatoes
4 vine tomatoes
1 slice watermelon

optional, for the homemade noodle pots:
bok choy
carrots
chillies
edamame beans
limes
mushrooms
spring greens
spring onions
mangetout

CUPBOARD
4 bread rolls
2 x 400g (14oz) cans butter beans
400g (14oz) can chickpeas
350g (12oz) self-raising wholemeal flour
1 tablespoon honey
udon, glass or Singapore-style noodles

250g (9oz) Arborio rice
2 reduced-salt vegetable stock cubes
bicarbonate of soda
plain flour
olive oil
olive oil spray
small tub olives
icing sugar
vegetable oil

REFRIGERATOR
400ml (14fl oz) buttermilk
150g (5½oz) Cheddar cheese
20g (¾oz) Parmesan cheese
200g (7oz) chicken breast
6 tablespoons soured cream
8 eggs
1 small tub hummus
270ml (9½fl oz) whole milk
slightly salted butter

optional, for the homemade noodle pots:
boiled eggs
cooked meat
firm tofu

HERBS & SPICES
chilli powder
large bunch coriander
ground coriander
ground cumin
garlic granules
smoked paprika
parsley
ground turmeric

WEEK 2

FRUIT & VEGETABLES
5–6 bananas
½ boiled beetroot
20g (¾oz) pickled beetroots
100g (3½oz) frozen mixed berries
40g (1½oz) red cabbage
2 carrots
½ large or 1 small courgette
60g (2¼oz) cucumber
1½ lemons
1 yellow pepper
1 pineapple

1 handful baby spinach
350g (12oz) strawberries
50g (1¾oz) cherry tomatoes

CUPBOARD
8 slices wholemeal bread
2 tablespoons cocoa powder
1 small jar pickled ginger
2 tablespoons granola
200g (7oz) cooked Puy lentils
3 tablespoons maple syrup
4 nori (dried seaweed) sheets
200g (7oz) rolled oats
30g (1oz) olives
250g (9oz) sushi rice
4 teaspoons sesame seeds
50g (1¾oz) sun-dried tomatoes in oil
4 tablespoons rice vinegar
1 tube wasabi paste
plain flour
olive oil
olive oil spray
vegetable oil
reduced-salt soy sauce
caster sugar

REFRIGERATOR
30g (1oz) feta cheese
50g (1¾oz) cream cheese
4 eggs
1 small tub hummus
940ml (1½ pints) whole milk
60g (2¼oz) smoked salmon
400g (14oz) natural yogurt

HERBS & SPICES
mint
vanilla extract

PHASE 4

WEEK 1

FRUIT & VEGETABLES
2 green apples
480g (1lb 1oz) butternut squash
3 carrots
½ fennel bulb

3 garlic cloves
2cm (¾in) fresh root ginger
1 lemon
1½ red onion
1 white onion
2 ripe peaches
2 firm pears
4 ripe plums
200g (7oz) potatoes
1 small bag salad leaves
300g (10½oz) strawberries

CUPBOARD
4 bagels
4 seeded buns
365g (12½oz) wholemeal flour
4 sheets (170g/6oz) fresh lasagne sheets
300g (10½oz) macaroni pasta
10g (¼oz) walnuts
baking powder
balsamic glaze
bicarbonate of soda
plain flour
mango chutney
olive oil
olive oil spray
vegetable oil

REFRIGERATOR
70g (2½oz) Parmesan cheese
250g (9oz) ricotta cheese
300g (10½oz) smoked cheese
300g (10½oz) crème fraîche
6 eggs
450ml (16fl oz) semi-skimmed milk
500ml (18fl oz) whole milk
slightly salted butter

HERBS & SPICES
chilli powder
fresh coriander
ground cinnamon
ground coriander
ground cumin
garlic granules
a few sprigs mint
whole nutmeg
parsley
thyme

WEEK 2

FRUIT & VEGETABLES
3 avocados
4 bananas
7 cloves, or ½ bulb, garlic
1 lime
500g (1lb 2oz) button mushrooms
400g (14oz) fresh or frozen okra
1½ red onions
3 white onions
1 green pepper
½ red pepper
2 tablespoons pomegranate seeds
300g (10½oz) tomatoes

CUPBOARD
80g (2¾oz) canned ackee
400g (14oz) can black beans
10 small, soft tortillas
130g (5oz) dried breadcrumbs
100g (3½oz) bulgur wheat
400g (14oz) can chickpeas
2 teaspoons cocoa powder
400g (14oz) can coconut milk
250g (9oz) self-raising wholemeal flour
300g (10½oz) strong white bread flour
200g (7oz) Puy lentils
100g (3½oz) red lentils
2 tablespoons maple syrup
2 teaspoons white miso paste
200g (7oz) rolled oats
200g (7oz) brown rice
½ tablespoon poppy seeds
2 tablespoons pumpkin seeds
50g (1¾oz) sunflower seeds
2 reduced-salt vegetable stock cubes
325g (11½oz) can sweetcorn
1 tablespoon tomato purée
200g (7oz) can chopped tomatoes
50g (1¾oz) sun-dried tomatoes in oil
bicarbonate of soda
black food colouring
plain flour
tomato ketchup
olive oil
olive oil spray
vegetable oil
peanut butter
fast-action dried yeast

REFRIGERATOR
60g (2¼oz) Cheddar cheese
50g (1¾oz) feta cheese
125g (4½oz) mozzarella cheese
4 tablespoons soured cream
8 eggs
400ml (14fl oz) whole milk
400g (14oz) natural yogurt

HERBS & SPICES
basil
fresh coriander
curry leaves
chilli powder
chilli flakes
ground coriander
ground cumin
cumin seeds
mint
mustard seeds
smoked paprika
parsley
ground turmeric
vanilla extract

PHASE 5

WEEK 1

FRUIT & VEGETABLES
2 avocados
2 bananas
1 head broccoli
200g (7oz) Tenderstem broccoli
150g (5½oz) butternut squash
½ red cabbage
140g (5oz) cucumbers
2 garlic cloves
1 lemon
1 mango
1 white onion
1 red pepper
1 small or ½ medium pineapple
1kg (2lb 4oz) Maris Piper potatoes
150g (5½oz) baby spinach
150g (5½oz) sweet potato

CUPBOARD
30g (1oz) dried apricots

4 pitta breads
1 small bottle chilli or sweet chilli sauce
50g (1¾oz) milk chocolate chips
30g (1oz) dried cranberries
3 tablespoons honey
20g (¾oz) oat bran
160g (5¾oz) rolled oats
15g (½oz) pine nuts
30g (1oz) dried pineapple
35g (1¼oz) pumpkin seeds
1 teaspoon sesame seeds
50g (1¾oz) sunflower seeds
20g (¾oz) wheat bran
plain flour
olive oil
olive oil spray
vegetable oil

REFRIGERATOR
200ml (7fl oz) apple juice
125g (4½oz) mozzarella cheese
12 cooked falafel
1 small tub hummus
6 tablespoons mayonnaise
100ml (3½fl oz) whole milk
200g (7oz) smoked sausage
125g (4½oz) natural yogurt
slightly salted butter

HERBS & SPICES
dill
mint
parsley
packet sage
chilli flakes

WEEK 2

FRUIT & VEGETABLES
½ avocado
2 heads bok choy
2 carrots
1 stick celery
1 red chilli
280g (10oz) cucumbers
2 garlic cloves
5cm (2in) fresh root ginger
100g (3½oz) mangetout
1 white onion
450g (1lb) parsnips

1 red pepper
250g (9oz) potatoes
8 radishes
160g (5¾oz) baby spinach
3 spring onions
100g (3½oz) baby sweetcorn
2 tomatoes

CUPBOARD
4 crusty bread rolls
50g (1¾oz) cashew nuts
500g (1lb 2oz) strong wholemeal bread flour
250g (9oz) soba noodles
1 tablespoon mixed nuts and seeds
100g (3½oz) pine nuts
160g (5¾oz) quinoa
4 rice cakes
4 teaspoons pumpkin seeds
1 tablespoon sesame seeds
4 teaspoons sunflower seeds
1 reduced-salt chicken stock cube
1 reduced-salt vegetable stock cube
1½ teaspoons caster sugar
plain flour
olive oil
olive oil spray
vegetable oil
reduced-salt soy sauce
white wine vinegar
fast-action dried yeast

REFRIGERATOR
2 cooked bacon rashers
125g (4½oz) mozzarella cheese
11 eggs
1 small tub hummus
250g (9oz) cooked pork
4 cooked sausages

HERBS & SPICES
fresh coriander
chilli flakes
fennel seeds
five spice powder
rosemary
sage

INDEX

GLOSSARY

UK	US
Baking beans	Pie weights; can use dried beans as a substitute
Baking paper	Parchment paper
Beef burger	Hamburger
Beetroot	Beet
Bicarbonate of soda	Baking soda
Bolognese	Ragù
Butter beans	Lima beans
Caster sugar	Superfine sugar
Cavolo nero	Black kale; can substitute with green kale
Chestnut mushrooms	Cremini mushrooms
Chips/potato chips	Fries
Clingfilm	Plastic wrap
Coriander (the herb)	Cilantro
Cornflour	Cornstarch
Courgette	Zucchini
Dark chocolate	Semisweet chocolate
Double cream	Heavy cream
English mustard	Dry mustard
Fish fingers	Fish sticks
Grill/grilled	Broiler/broiled
Haricot beans	Navy beans
Icing sugar	Confectioners' sugar/powdered sugar
Kitchen paper	Paper towels
Lardons	Bacon pieces
Lolly	Ice pop
Low-salt	Low-sodium
Mangetout	Snow peas
Maris Piper potatoes	Yukon gold potatoes
Mixed spice	Substitute with allspice
Plain flour	All-purpose flour
Porridge	Oatmeal
Quorn	Textured vegetable protein
Rocket	Arugula
Runner beans	Green beans
Scone	Similar to a dinner biscuit
Self-rising flour	Use all-purpose flour plus 1 tsp baking powder per 4½oz (1 cup) flour
Semi-skimmed milk	Low-fat milk
Soldiers	Strips of toast
Spring greens	Collard greens
Spring onion	Scallion
Sprouting broccoli	Broccolini
Stock cube	Bouillon cube
Swede	Rutabaga
Sweetcorn	Corn/corn kernels
Toad-in-the-hole	Link-style sausages baked in batter
Tomato purée	Tomato paste
Veg crisps	Vegetable chips
Wholemeal	Whole-wheat

ACKNOWLEDGEMENTS

Writing a cookery book is at once a solitary endeavour and a team sport. As much as you're holed up alone in a study or kitchen, you're also calling on friends and family for all manner of support. Without feedback, without encouragement, without draft readers, pasta-tasters and chapter-debaters it would be an almost impossible task.

In particular, I must thank:

Mark for endless washing up, cups of tea, taste-testing, patience, love and encouragement. He is one in eight billion.

Maeve for being the most patient, kind, intelligent woman I know and one hell of a mum. There is nothing I could say to adequately express my gratitude.

Jay and JD, my willing (and sometimes unwilling) guinea pigs; my inspiration and self-appointed cheerleaders on the road from concept to book.

OB, who worked tirelessly alongside me, creatively and organizationally, from first to last. Whip smart and a gem of a human.

Madelaine, my best friend, who placed my first-ever published article as a food writer, and who shares my penchant for strange working hours.

My followers on amummytoo.co.uk, Instagram, Twitter, Facebook and Pinterest, whose constant support, feedback, ideas, photos, stories and questions remind me daily why I do what I do.

And finally, my blogging family, especially Ciara, Grace, Helene, Charlotte, Mel, Hannah, Helen, Donna, Michael, Becky and Penny. Much love x